Delicacy of the gods

Delicacy of the gods

A. Abeku Haywood-Dadzie

Delicacy of the gods
Copyright © 2024, A. Abeku Haywood-Dadzie

ISBN: 978-9988-3-7647-5

Edited by Angeline Addy,
WriteRight Editing Services

Layout design and e-book digitising by Sam Nyarko-Mensah
Cover design by Ben Apaw

I dedicate this book to
Madam Henrittah Tetteh, my late mother,
who never ceased to inspire me and gave me
confidence that I could do anything in life.
I guess she was right.

PROLOGUE

About seven kilometres from Ada-Foah on a tortuous, undulating ramp-like road is a pot-shaped town dominated by giant coconut trees, colourful birds, wildflowers, and marked tombstones. This beautiful town of Tofekope is bordered by an estuarine shoreline on the northeast and a marine coastline on the southeast. A bird's-eye view from the coconut trees on the Aplabaya road presents a peaceful paradise with a serene atmosphere.

The charming hamlet of Mukope, formerly referred to as the "garden of the gods," is close to Tofekope, a place with an abundance of flora and fauna and breathtaking beaches along its southeasterly coastline. The island is encircled by a horseshoe plateau that kisses the sea at the heel. The town's rivers, lakes, and lagoons are divided into vegetation assemblages. Mukope prospered during the Gold Coast era due to the trade in "white gold" (salt). Nene Momo, the Mukope chief, was the state's head of justice and religion and an absolute monarch. The town flourished and expanded thanks to an elite army with cavalry units and access to raw materials such as iron ore to make its weapons and salt deposits to pay its soldiers. The chief always had absolute control over the salt mines; no one else could own salt mines in Mukope. In this way, he controlled the supply to avoid a glut. During his reign, the great chief built a tremendously rich empire by implementing clever reforms and improvements, such as enhancing defence capabilities, growing the royal court, and reaping the benefits of more effective and smart taxation. He had labour conscriptions from adjacent Tofekope and Muteh, tributes and gifts from distant towns, and a land and sea commercial system that relied on a robust army to safeguard its assets and trade routes.

Following the demise of the renowned chief Nene Momo, his son's leadership failed the once proud and prosperous town. Nene Sakitey, the new chief of Mukope, did not only engage in frivolous battles but also superintended over a corrupt administration. He formed useless alliances, leading to betrayal, which led to the final collapse of the town. Nene Sakitey was the epitome of immorality. One of his frivolous wars eventually resulted in the downfall of Mukope, which even became a vassal state to Tofekope, which once owed allegiance to Mukope. Even though it is a forbidden subject in public discourse, Nene Sakitey's insistence on marrying the wife of Tofekope 's linguist—because he had seen the woman bathing by the riverside and couldn't resist his urge—was one of the remote causes that ultimately resulted in war and Mukope becoming a vassal state. His insistence on marrying another man's wife was the unforeseen path that led to a terrifying battle between the two towns. In the end, the wise counsel of one of the veteran soldiers who had returned from the war in Burma led to the defeat of Mukope; hence, they became a vassal state of Tofekope.

Modernity has done little to change current-day Tofekope; it is enslaved by traditions and customs that haven't changed over the years due to the stranglehold particular people have on the inhabitants. These characters with entrenched positions operate selfishly, to the detriment of the community's progress. The "Delicacy of the Gods" is the story of a young girl, Doeyo, whose entire life was impacted by the actions of both the spiritual and physical forces that rule in the community, with Ayeku playing a significant role in it. What is their individual ancestry, and how do their lives intertwine?

WHO IS DOEYO?

Doeyo's existence is as captivating as her beauty. Her grandparents were Papa Pateh and Mama Kabutey. Papa Pateh was one of the elegant soldiers from the Gold Coast who joined the Royal West African Frontier Force; 1st Battalion Gold Coast Regiment, to fight alongside the British Army in Burma. On returning home, he became a leading activist who carried out several civil disobedience operations against the colonial government and the activities of the Association of West African Merchants (AWAM), one of which later culminated in the February 1948 Riot. Papa Pateh was a gentleman's gentleman, always looking dapper. Every February 28th was a special day in his family house, and, by extension in the community. That was the day Papa Pateh would don his khaki drill, red fez, sleeveless scarlet Zouave-style jacket edged in yellow, and red cummerbunds to join his colleagues in the big city to commemorate the anniversary of the deaths of three of the ex-soldiers.

The soldiers were killed after police broke up a civil disobedience by some of his comrades who were agitating for their rights as World War II veterans. All promises made to these veterans upon their return to the Gold Coast had been reneged on by the man whose name is a "taboo on our lips" - the man from a distant shore.

Mama Kabutey was a beautiful, clever, humble, and friendly lady who worked as a nurse in the big cities while her husband was stationed in Burma. At one point in time, she was recruited as an attaché nurse to the 1st Battalion Nigeria Regiment and also served as the head of the Red Cross in East Africa. Subsequently, Papa Pateh became the court registrar, and Mama Kabutey set up a chemist at the edge of the town. The couple had an only child, Doe, born a few years after the 1948 riot at the Princess Marie Louise Hospital in Accra, the big city. Doe spent little time in Tofekope; most of her education was in Accra. She was one of the few "standard six" graduates who were selected and trained by scholarship at the Prince of Wales College, Achimota, by the newly elected administration of the Gold Coast.

Doe was a born leader and an intelligent woman who became head of one of the new schools in the capital city. During one vacation, when visiting her parents, Doe met one of the merchants from Tofekope. A whirlwind romance ensued, leading to a polygamous marriage and the birth of Doeyo, whose existence is shrouded in mystery; rumour has it that she was not born of the purported father, the richest merchants in Tofekope. Whispers gave her paternity to the old fetish priest, who played a significant role in her mother's life during her conception.

WHO IS AYEKU?

The town of Tofekope was ruled by a great chief who had two children, Nene Ku and Nene Kai. Customarily, the elder Nene Ku should have succeeded his father to the throne, but he refused. Christened Bright Wisdom Acolatse, Nene Ku, was a highly intelligent young man who was accepted to Oxford University, where he earned an LL.B., a post-graduate scholarship, and a master's degree. He practiced for a while in England after being admitted to the English Bar. He was born chief of his people, but much to his father's dismay, he refused to return to the Gold Coast to assume that responsibility because he did not want to be in charge of a band of "savages" in a historic settlement. The great chief deployed all available means of persuasion, including moving to London to convince Bright Wisdom Acolatse to return home, but he would not budge. After a protracted period of mental anguish over this blasphemy, the great chief's health declined, he fell ill, and he eventually died in England. Even though Nene Ku returned with the body of the eminent chief to Tofekope, he had no interest in remaining and departed for England to carry on with his legal career and enjoy his reputation as a counsellor par excellence after the funeral.

After two years without a chief, the people of Tofekope installed his younger brother, Nene Kai, to succeed his father. A few years later, Nene Ku returned home and became one of the key advocates of the Association of West African Merchants (AWAM).

This put Doeyo's grandfather and young Nene Ku at odds because the grandfather was involved in civil disobedience activities against the AWAM group. However, years later, they were able to patch up their differences when Nene Ku finally returned to settle in Tofekope and worked at the courthouse where Doeyo's grandfather served as the court registrar. The truce, however, was short-lived because Nene Ku was constantly involved in dishonest court cases and exploited the community by using his royal ancestry. He used his legal acumen to swindle and repossess most of the land belonging to the community. The height of his irresponsible behaviour was when he decided to ascend the very throne he had earlier rejected. Nene Ku had no moral compass; he used his wealth and knowledge to destroy a lot of homes. Though he never married, he accepted one child as his— Ayeku.

* * *

Doeyo was developing into a lovely young woman who delighted the gods and attracted the covert and overt lust of mortal men (both affluent and impoverished in Tofekope). Doeyo was special from the start. When she was younger, she was the talk of the town. Over time, she grew beautifully and became the town's main attraction. She was the target of the town's aristocratic and less privileged suitors. The chief, the fetish priest, the teacher, the prophet, wealthy men, and Ayeku were just a few of the many men who wanted to marry her.

The sudden assignment of the new teacher, a national serviceman to the town, caused issues because he uses his classroom activities to explain the causes of most local natural occurrences deemed acts of the gods by the town and its priest. This was a problem for some of the elders in the town. While some elders of the town supported the young teacher because of their own parochial interests, others fought him for his outlook on redundant customary practices.

LIST OF CHARACTERS

Main Characters

Chief: Overlord of Puteh

Linguist: Spokesman for the chief

Town Crier: The ever-inebriated announcer of the palace

Prophet: The representative of the Christian God who has an unhealthy hold on the townsfolk

Priest: The Fetish or traditional priest of Tofekope has the whole town in his grip. The main beneficiary of the Trokosi system, he is always ready to add to his harem.

Teacher: The senior teacher of the local school

Mensa: A young man

Ayeku: A despicable young man with royal leanings

Livingston: A young teacher posted for national service at Tofekope incurs the ire of some townsfolk as he uses classroom activities to explain the causes of most local natural occurrences.

Doeyo: A beautiful, intriguing young girl who dares to go against tradition, advocating strongly for the abolition of the dehumanising practices of Trokosi and female genital mutilation.

Women of Tofekope:
Mama Owe
Mama Doe
Mama Sacketey
Mama Naa
Mama Ogbo
Mama Yaa
Mama Saa
Mama Dey

Young girls:
Aku
Korkor
Dedei

It is a beautiful morning, and the sun is hanging low in the brilliant blue sky. Some menfolk can be seen leaving the lagoon site, trailed by their children toting decorated head pans with fishing nets. Those folks who visited "the noisy neighbour" can be seen dragging their nets from its belly with highly rhythmic singing. The women, with their clothes wrapped around their body from the breast to the knee and tied just above their breasts, can be seen swaying their waists artfully in rhythm to the songs.

Standing by the shore and smiling coyly at the menfolk are a group of pregnant teenagers who chose to explore their newfound womanhood at a tender age. With towels in hand, they are ready to clean off the curse inflicted on man by Odomankoma. Per the instructions of the Prophet of the Almighty Odomankoma, they are to clean their sweats with the towels for disobedience.

In another scene, the pupils at the school are involved in various activities. Two friends are freely expressing themselves in the language of "He whose name is a taboo," with questionable grammar.

SCENE 1

A New Teacher in Town

Two friends are conversing erroneously in the language of "He whose name is a taboo, "not too far from the school compound, where pupils are busy cleaning the compound and getting ready for lessons.

Mensa: Today the teacher was not going to come to school.

Ayeku: Are you true?

Mensa: Can I false you?

Meanwhile, at the Mission House
Seated under the big old Odum tree in front of the church, which is opposite the chief's palace and adjacent to the school, is the ubiquitous Prophet, dressed in colourful vestments, with the Bible in his right hand fixed firmly on his heart, while he receives greetings as well as the "tithe" of his "sheep's returns." The town crier passes by and calls out a greeting. The linguist soon followed the prophet with a young man in town.

Linguist: Greetings, the Lord's Anointed, please, how are you doing? And Mama Prophet, how are the children and the entire household? Your servants are here to visit you.

Livingston: Greetings, sir *(smiling as they shake hands in turn)*.

Prophet: Good day, my sons *(turning to the linguist)*; everybody is doing well by the grace of Odomankoma. Eheh! Before I forget, thank you for the invaluable number of mudfish, crabs, and tilapia you sent to me. I'm sorry, but the name of your daughter, whom you sent, has slipped my mind.

Linguist: Ama.

Prophet: Eheeh Ama. She has grown into a pretty young lady. It is strange how fast these young ones are growing now. I'm sure she will be betrothed very soon, and your efforts will pay off in a dowry. Anyway, how is everything back at home? Your wives and concubines—I hope everybody is fine.

Linguist: Yes! Everybody is fine. Since we are enjoying the mercies of Odomankoma, we can't complain.

Prophet: How about you, young man?

Livingston: I'm fine, sir.

Prophet: *(He stretches his hand and greets the young man.)* Anyway, everything is fine here. Odomankoma has blessed us with another beautiful day. After going about my duties in the church, Linguist, as you know, the scripture says, "Seek ye first the kingdom of God," I decided to sit here and admire Odomankoma's creations. As the elders say, everything is fine here. As my guest, I shall still inquire, even though I am aware of the motive for this visit. You are welcome.

Linguist: Thank you, the Lord's anointed prophet. Once again, everything is fine where we come from, and thank you so much for appreciating my offering. Odomankoma has indeed been good to us. But, as to why we are here, I believe you have been seeing this young man in town for some time now. He is our new teacher from the big city, and he's come to assist Teacher Ako at the Totomekope School Complex. He will be here for a year. He is undertaking his national duty, what has come to be known as "national suffering." Prophet, you may recall that we had the privilege of hosting a "mermaid" last year.

Livingston: (*Interrupts*) A mermaid? Please, it's a national service internship. (*National Service is a compulsory one-year service required of all who have completed tertiary education.*)

Linguist: (Laughs) Sorry, I stand corrected. What I meant was that the national service teacher was so beautiful, and she ended up bringing tragedy to the men in this town. Anyway, they have themselves to blame. As I was saying, Holy One, now we have this young man here to undertake his national suffering.

Livingston: (*Interrupts*) It's national service, my linguist.

Linguist: Thank you, national service.

Prophet: You are welcome, my son. Thanks for accepting the duty to serve in this town and to help educate our children. May Odomankoma bless you.

Linguist: (*Continues*) Since you are one of the most respected elders in this community, and as per our elders' saying, "Those who respect the elderly create their own route towards success," the chief thought it proper to introduce him to you first and to inform you of the date of his outdooring. The Chief will introduce him to the people in the town at the grand durbar.

Prophet: Wonderful!What wonderful news! That is really excellent of you, linguist. (*He turns to the young man.*) Welcome, my son. "When a bird flies off the earth and lands on an anthill, it is still on the ground." Welcome home. I pray everyone is well where you are coming from, especially your family, wives, and concubines.

Livingston: (*The young man stands up and shakes the hand of the prophet.*) Everyone is fine where

I am coming from, the Lord's Anointed, and they all send their greetings. (Smiles). However, I am not yet married and do not have concubines.

Prophet: *(Turning towards the young man)* Tell me, my son, are you sure? Knowing that I am a prophet, you should not keep any secrets from me because the Lord will expose your deception if you do. He won't keep anything from folks like us; I'm sure you know that. Besides, I'm convinced you are aware that if you travel in deceit, you will arrive at your destination, but you might not be able to go back in the same direction.

Livingston: *(Smiles)* It's true, and I don't intend to hide anything from you, sir.

> *(Worried that the conversation would get off course, the linguist interjects.)*

Linguist: He is Kweku Livingston and comes from the town where "He whose name is a taboo" first settled when they arrived and took our ancestors and their gods into slavery in an unknown land, to be precise, Babylon. Yes, when they relocated our gods to Babylon.

Prophet: Linguist, where did you hear about Babylon? Anyway, what a shame; I guess he comes from... what's the name? Gua, er... Oguaa, shame.Anyway, *(facing the young man)*, I visited the dungeons when I was a young seminarian; I could not believe the wickedness "He whose name is a taboo" showed to our ancestors. Man's inhumanity to man — it was so atrocious (he picks up the handkerchief and starts wiping tears).

Livingston: You are correct, sir *(not sure where this is going)*. My, my, parents are from Cape Coast. My apologies for the emotional trauma the name of my town brings. But you are right.

Prophet: (He cleans his face with a big towel.) Anyway, you have been calling me "sir." I'm not, sir. That was the name used by "He whose name is a taboo." They deceived our forefathers by not giving us their real names. Isn't it because Odomankoma doesn't like wickedness that he gave every creature a name for the purpose of identification? Instead, they asked our people to call them sirs and twisted the tenets of the good book so they could roll out their evil deeds. I'm the Prophet, the Holy One, the Lord's Anointed, and the man Odomankoma has appointed to lead this town to Zion. You see! The fact that the millipede and the snake both move on their bellies does not mean they are related.

Livingston: Yes, sir. Apologies, sir. *(He fumbles.)* Please pardon my slip of the tongue.

Prophet: You better tame it, my son. You better tame that tongue *(smiles)*. My scripture reading this morning says, "Whoever would love life and see good days must keep their tongue." *(Turning to the linguist.)* I believe Peter said that, linguist, or not? *(He continues before the linguist responds.)* Why am I even asking you when you have not darkened the doorway of the church for months? *(He turns to the young man.)* Anyway, let me ask: What exactly did you bring from the city that is so appealing to the young people in this town? You know, a tasty soup invites seats. Their side of the pew in the church hasn't been warmed up since you moved to this community, and this has impacted church activities. *(He giggles.)* I sincerely hope you did not bring the "eye" of He-whose-name-is-taboo with you or his culture.

Livingston: *(Trying to return the smile.)* Nothing! No, sir; I mean, Holy One. I find it very difficult to drive them away from my home when they visit. But if I know the time for the church service, I will do my best to send them to the house of God.

Prophet: You would have to find a way of persuading them to attend church, I suppose. I sincerely hope you are not one of the self-propagating individuals who come to this town with their skewed Holy Ghost beliefs. Is the Holy Father a ghost? That will be the topic of a different conversation, though.

Livingston: Absolutely not, sir. Despite my belief in the Holy Ghost, sir, I'm not the self-propagating sort. Sorry, I meant Holy One.

Prophet: *(Not quite happy, but trying to force a smile. He turns to the linguist.)* I guess the introduction is done, then. I will find Teacher Ako so that we can help in the planning of the durbar. But you better find the town crier who can't stay off the "major glass" of that "blue kiosk" to announce the durbar date to the townsfolk.

Linguist: I'll do that, please, Holy One. *(He stands up and shakes the prophet's hand; Livingston does likewise.)* If there's nothing more to be considered, we'll beg to take our leave now.

Prophet: *(He smiles.)* Young man, have you brought anything from the city for me? Considering the fact that you are coming from the town where "He whose name is a taboo" first arrived, I know you brought me some whisky and toffees. I have no doubt that this is what prevents our young people from attending church.

Livingston: No, sir! Sorry, I intend to say Holy One.

Prophet: Okay, Linguist and young man, er, Livingston, thank you. But Linguist, there is a discussion we need to have about the people of the next town, but that would be another day.

Linguist: Prophet, I would make myself available anytime.

Prophet: Let's pray then. *(He quoted the scripture.)*

"The LORD bless you and keep you,

The LORD, make His face shine upon you,

And be gracious to you.

The LORD lift up His countenance upon you,

And give you peace."

He stretches his hand over them and says, Go with God.

The linguist leads Livingston out of the house through the main gate of the church. Soon they are on the road that leads them to the school premises.

Linguist: You two appear to be off to a bad start. Have you spoken to him previously or before this visit?

Livingston: Certainly not. I have walked past him perhaps twice in my early morning stroll for fresh air, as he leisurely walked barefoot in the sea sand. And it isn't as if I ignore him; I always wish him a good morning, but it appears I have already offended him.

Linguist: Then, you must exercise extreme caution. He is an expert at complicating straightforward issues and a real genius at making simple issues complex.

Livingston: What do you mean when you say he has a knack for making simple issues complex?

Linguist: My son, I won't repeat it. I really, really mean what I said. Don't get excited. The ear that listens to counsel is not as big as a basket. (He paused and looked at him.) Besides, based just on appearance, you seem to be highly ambitious, which is a concern because when you are overly ambitious, you may not be able to sleep soundly at night.

Livingston: *(ignores the comments from the linguist)* I appreciate the hospitality I've already experienced so far from the town folk and your guidance.

Linguist: Hospitality or hostility—that's not my business. But keep your distance from his radar eyes and razor-sharp tongue. (He whispers something to him.) You don't go shaking hands with a porcupine. Your eyes may not have seen what he is capable of doing, but believe your ears when you are told.

Livingston: I'm lucky to have some of the townsfolk on my side.

Linguist: *(Sounds angry now.)* I don't think so. You are beginning to sound like the former District Chief Executive who was assigned to this town not long ago and had sticks in his ears. If you care to know, his end was very miserable. The disease that will kill a man first break sticks into the ears. Though you may have large eyes, keep in mind that you are a stranger and that you may not be able to see everything. Besides, why don't you hold off on declaring yourself lucky until misfortune passes you by? Life's riddles have different meanings depending on the language you speak and how you perceive what's conveyed. Okay, see you around *(they parted ways).*

SCENE 2
The "Outdooring" of Livingston

Days later. The durbar to introduce Livingston, the new teacher, is being held at the school, which is an impressive piece by all standards. A majestic structure with well-manicured green grass, bordered by coconut trees whitewashed at the waist. It is a sunny, dry, and dusty Tuesday. The harmattan clouds cast a pale hue over the town, and the whistling echoes of the wind can be heard all around. There is no fishing activity since it is the second day of the work week. Just like the majority of the coastal communities of Ghana, Tuesday is a day of rest and taking stock of life's challenges for the townsfolk. People have crowded every inch of the school compound for the colourful durbar. The occasion is full of traditional pomp, pageantry, and gaiety. Amidst intense drumming, singing, and dancing, the chiefs and queen mothers ride in procession in their gorgeous traditional palanquins. The durbar is not so much an occasion to welcome the new teacher to Tofekope as it is a ceremony to honour the ancestors, rekindle their bond with the people, revive unity, and cleanse the town. Seated at centre stage on the podium is the chief, flanked by his able lieutenants. The Prophet and Teacher Ako sit on the right; Livingston sits next to him, while the seats on the left are occupied by the linguist, the fetish priest, and some elders of the town.

The pupils from the school start their performance; the drums burst forth with a rhythmic chiming, and it is simply beautiful to watch pupils move their feet and other parts of their bodies in beautiful rhythm—they sprint, stoop, stamp, swing, and sway their bodies in perfect unison. They are tastefully dressed in traditional clothes with matching colourful beads. Their foreheads, shoulders, necks, and ankles are skillfully painted with traditional body art made with white chalk.

Dancing exceptionally well, Doeyo, the beautiful damsel, leads the pupils. She seems to have taken centre stage with her well-coordinated bodily movements and smiles. Her performance is impressive, and the new teacher is really feeling honoured. You could hear them sing:

> "Wogbɛ jɛkɛ e, ejɛkɛ jɛkɛ, wɔjɛ shɔn.
> Wogbɛ jɛkɛ e, ejɛkɛ jɛkɛ, wɔjɛ shɔn.
> Wogbɛ jɛkɛ e, ejɛkɛ jɛkɛ, wɔjɛ shɔn.
> Wogbɛ jɛkɛ e, ejɛkɛ jɛkɛ, wɔjɛ shɔn.
>
> Kɛjɛ Israel kɛba Egypt, kɛba Ethiopia kɛ
>   Sudan, wɔjɛ shɔn.
> Kɛjɛ Ayikushi man yi nɔ, wɔ Nii mei kɛ wɔ
>   Naa mei, wɔjɛ shɔn.
> Soso, Timbuktu, Ghana, Mali, Sumanguru yi
>   nɔ, wɔjɛ shɔn.
> Wogbɛ jɛkɛ e, ejɛ ke jɛkɛ, wɔjɛ shɔn.

Mensa and his friend are also at the Durbar grounds.

Mensa: *(Swaying in dance.)* Doeyo is gorgeous, especially with her seductive looks, elegant clothing, and captivating grin. She has never before appeared to be so joyful. She is breath-takingly exquisite.

Ayeku: Who said she came here to dance? Just observe how she smiles and exchanges glances with that "small boy-big man" they call Livingston. Look, look, just take a quick peek, just like the sunflower tracing the path of the rising sun.

Mensa: And so, what? Who cares? Remember, there's no medicine that can cure hatred. The group is here to honour Livingston, our new teacher, so she must act appropriately as their leader.

Ayeku: *(Dissatisfied.)* Who? That nocturnal stranger? That weird midnight visitor! The camouflage of "He whose name is a taboo". Look! Just look at how they reciprocate romantic smiles. Never before has she grinned at me in this manner.

Mensa: Don't be paranoid, my brother. Her grin is required. Some events are so fascinating and exciting that they transcend conventional behavioural patterns. She must be delighted to see Livingston, her new teacher. And as you can see, Livingston does not appear to be harmful like Teacher Ako, who has a chain of concubines, yet the prophet says he is the divine choice for the position of town treasurer. Again, according to rumours, the new teacher observes morning devotions and quiet time exactly like our late headmaster instructed us to. He is said to be calm, innocent, innocuous, inoffensive, and nontoxic.

Ayeku: *(Frowning.)* Did you, by any chance, swallow an undigested dictionary? Spare me, for God's sake, the sermon on morality. I believe the fetish priest, with his broken moral compass, needs it more than I do.

Mensa: Do I sound choked? You better stop this sacred mockery. I have just been reading the books I picked from Livingston! He has a lot of such books. Let me introduce you to him after the durbar so you can borrow some.

Ayeku: *(Looking at him in dismay.)* Thankfully, I won't have to stop watching the romantic scene Livingston and his pupils are enacting in order to get you some water. However, heed this warning: Never assume that when the water is calm, crocodiles are absent. *(He pauses and takes another look at Mensa.)* And Mensa, perhaps you are not aware of this; the crocodile frequently claims that while it is shy to bite, it is also shy to release its bite. Regardless of how he looks or whether he is harmful or not, worms can be found even in unripe pepper.

Mensa: What is going on? Why have you become jealous all of a sudden? You've been with her since she was a baby, and you're constantly up against her. Why the sudden envy? If it is love, then this kind of love is quite odd. Remember, a man who hangs around a beautiful lady he loves without saying a word will end up fetching water for guests at her wedding.

Ayeku: Why shouldn't I be jealous, eh? Even weeds get greedy whenever the rainy season is nearby. Besides, it is only a fool who keeps a flock of chickens all year long and then cheerfully takes them to the neighbour's cooking pot for the festive occasion.

Mensa: Ayeku, I beg you to stop! You should have been more knowledgeable and aware that when the hunter continuously brings home mushrooms instead of meat to toast the maiden because he doesn't understand how fierce the competition for her is, he shouldn't get upset when others bring elephant meat to her. You need to develop the habit of treating the woman you love with respect. Bear in mind that nobody will buy your head if you don't put it up for sale.

(They keep quiet for a while and watch what is going on.)

Ayeku: "Even the chief of the forest, the lion, protects himself against flies." I'm surprised by your ignorance and naive remarks on a subject on which you have limitations. You've never been in a romantic relationship. If you had, you would have understood that the quarrel of lovers is simply the renewal of love.

Mensa: You're right. I've never been in this situation before, I'll be honest, my brother, but you seem to be forcing love on the young woman because you're afraid of reason;

in this circumstance, the only way you'll
learn is by failing.

The linguist, Teacher Ako, fetish priest, prophet, and chief take turns speaking to the people and welcoming the young man. The durbar ends on an excellent note with an announcement of communal labour at the weekend. The whole town responds with applause and cheers of joy as some of the women spread their cloths on the ground for the young man to walk on.

SCENE 3
Lustful Encounters and Meaningful Gossip

Crowd disperses. Some of the young ladies are discussing what happened at the Durbar grounds.

Aku: Oh! The new teacher is very handsome. Did you see his curly hair and muscles? And his… Oh, I'm in love with him already.

Korkor: Stop being such a shameless woman. Do you not have any shame? You are a married woman! During the queen mother's outdooring a couple of weeks ago, you were the same person gallantly parading your husband for all to see. So why this level of immorality?

Dedei: Korkor, what's your problem? So, doesn't she have the right to admire anyone else, eh? Korkor, it is said that an honest confession is difficult to make, but it brings liberation and peace to the soul and mind.

Korkor: Don't you think her husband will be jealous if he hears about this? Or is it just a matter of being immoral?

Dedei: Pretentious liar! Maybe you'll get jealous. Keep in mind that when a person acts as a traitor secretly, evil things happen to her in a similar manner. We won't swallow poison because we are afraid to spit and offend you. *(She turns to Aku.)* He's got a lot of hair on his chest and on his legs, which kills me the most. By the way, do you know if he is married?

Aku: No, but I hope he's not married.

Dedei: (Speak at the same time.) We will be ready to provide any service he requires, even if he...

Korkor: Even what? What exactly? *(Muttering to herself.)* Indeed, evil doesn't come from outside; it comes from within. (Aloud, she says), what exactly? *(Then she mutters to herself.)* Yes, indeed, evil doesn't come from outside; it comes from within, and as to him being married, I don't know, but one thing I know for sure is that this is mutually assured madness. I think it's time for you "old girls" to go home to your families and prepare food for them if you don't have any sensible issues to discuss.

Aku: Who said what we are discussing is not important? The fact that you are not married means nothing in this context. And why are you not married? Are we all not of the same age? Or you consider yourself to be self-sufficient, like the plantain plant?

Korkor: *(She ignores the comments on marriage.)* Old girls, I think you know that if a married woman decides to cook while also courting the most attractive bachelor in town simultaneously, either her food on the fire will burn or she'll return home with a broken face.

(Following them closely and eavesdropping on their conversation are Mensa and Ayeku.)

Ayeku: He has barely spent a month in this town, and look at the confusion his presence is already causing. I'm going to make sure that "small-boy, big-man," they call him sir, Livingston leaves this town immediately.

Mensa: You have a big mouth, I see. What prevents you from carrying it out? Additionally, who died and appointed you as our chief?

Ayeku: Your mother died and made me chief. Nonsense.

Mensa: Enough of such jokes, Ayeku.

Ayeku: Why? Do you think I'm amusing myself?

Mensa: Don't you think you're going too far with this youthful exuberance? You don't even know where he's from or what his traditions are, and yet you're already passing judgement on him.

Ayeku: Why are you trying to poke your nose into my affairs? I have told you to spare me the sermon on morality; your uncle needs it more.

Mensa: Please don't let your emotions overrule your judgement in whatever decisions you take.

Ayeku: I'm sorry. When did you become a counselor? Anyway, for your information, I trust my instincts.

(Just then, Doeyo runs towards them; she informs Ayeku that the prophet needs him.)

Doeyo: Hello, handsome young men, how was our dancing performance? Did you like it? Do you think Livingston liked it?

Mensa: Hello, my queen. You were beautiful, and you girls danced to perfection. Where did you all learn that?

(She only informs them she is going to prepare food for Livingston and darts off like a deer.)

Ayeku: I said it; that small boy-big man called Livingston will...

Mensa: What did you say? You never learned to appreciate what she does, yet you want her to fall in love with you. It's never done! She is not stoic.

(They part company, and Ayeku gets to the church to find the prophet kneeling down before the altar, shouting on top of his voice.)

Prophet: Praise the Lord! Praise Him in His sanctuary! Praise Him for His mighty firmament!

Ayeku: *(He enters and, as usual, decides to stand at the back.)* Amen.

Prophet: Praise Him according to His exceeding greatness!

Ayeku: Hallelujah!

Prophet: Praise Him with a trumpet sound!

Ayeku: Amen!

Prophet: Praise Him with flutes and harps.

Ayeku: Hallelujah!

Prophet: Praise Him with timbrels and dance!

Ayeku: Amen!

Prophet: Praise Him with strings and pipes!

Ayeku: Hallelujah!

Prophet: Praise Him with sounding cymbals!

Ayeku: Let everything that has breath praise the Lord.

Prophet: Praise Him by rolling on the beach.

Ayeku: *(Reluctantly.)* Yes, eh, by rolling

(The exaltation ends, and he walks towards the prophet.)

Ayeku: Your Lordship sent for me. Your servant is humbly before you, Anointed One. I am sorry for my inability to undertake my duties in the church this morning. The linguist employed us, the young men in the town, to prepare the school area for the durbar.

Prophet: "Seek ye first the kingdom of God." You know that. Son of Adam, you need deliverance.

Ayeku: Yes, I require deliverance, and I have brought the necessary funds.

Prophet: Seed of Adam, you need deliverance.

Ayeku: Yes, Prophet, I need deliverance.

Prophet: You therefore knoweth what to do; go ye therefore to the beach and roll a hundred times to the left and the same to the right. After that, do five Naaman dips and three of John's baptisms, and then come back to be anointed.

Ayeku: Oh, no! I just finished my penance for gambling this morning.

Prophet: Thus saith the Lord, "This time do all the hundred." The heavens opened, with angels ascending and descending while on the durbar ground. And I was caught up in the spirit. In the vision, I saw you swallowed by a fish like Jonah, leprous like Naaman, and blinded like Saul. Son of Adam, you need deliverance.

Ayeku: Yes! Yes! I require everything.

He leaves the prophet's presence and comes back about an hour later, his clothes filled with sand and water dripping out from every part of his body, panting like tilapia, which had just been taken out of the lagoon. As soon as the prophet sees him, he starts shouting again.

Prophet: Forgive him, Lord; forgive him, Lord! Create in him a clean heart; grant him a new life!

Ayeku: Yes, Lord, forgive me.

(The prophet then walks up to him and looks at him from head to toe.)

Prophet: Why, my son, are you following in the footsteps of your great-granduncle Cain? Why have you allowed the flames of hatred to burn so brightly in your soul?

Ayeku: Has the Lord forgiven me? Holy One, because I'm tired.

Prophet: *(He ignores the question.)* While at the durbar ground, you didn't only express your dislike for our new guest but also had a "horizontal relationship" with Doeyo.

Ayeku: No, I did not. No, I did not.

Prophet: You did, indeed.

Ayeku: No, sir.

Prophet: *(Astonished.)* Since when did you start calling me sir?

Ayeku: No, Prophet, I did nothing like that. Why? Has she been violated? Then it will be the new teacher, Livingston. Oh, no! But I just saw her. I never violated Doeyo. I do confess that I used to spy on her whenever she went to have her bath by the riverside, but you see, I'm engulfed in a ring of love, and there seems to be no way out. I hope you understand! I need her like the day needs the sun and the clouds need the sky. You understand, don't you, sir? Sir, I can't shy away from feeding my eyes; what the eyes see, especially when it comes to Doeyo, brings satisfaction to my soul.

Prophet: You're a moron, boy! You need nothing, like nothing. I am surprised at you! So you used to spy on her. My son, you need more than I ever imagined. *(Mutters)* Truly, it does not matter how the rain wets the leopard's spots; it will not be able to wash them off. As a crab walks, so do its children.

Ayeku: But I only spied on her, sir. You know, "Love makes a man blind and deaf."

Prophet: How dare you refer to me in that way again? How dare you call me by the name of "He whose name is a taboo"? Has that young man polluted you too? The devil wants you, my son. He has come in human form this time, and he seeks to devour you.

Ayeku: Please pray for me, sir. I mean, Prophet, I need your prayers.

Prophet: It seems "He whose name is a taboo" has come in another form and colour to devour our people.

Ayeku: How do you mean? You mean God is here with us? But you said there must be a rapture first.

Prophet: Don't you know "He whose name is a taboo" is? Another dumb remark. The man who invaded our nation from a distant continent took our heroes, tricked our ancestors, and, using mirrors, alcohol, and weapons *(muttering to himself)*, razed our sociopolitical system to the ground. The toffees they gave our ancestors-that is what really irritates me. Anyway, I love those toffees (he whispers to himself). They used it to fool and trick our ancestors. What are they currently teaching you, if I may ask?

Ayeku: *(He bursts into uncontrollable laughter, then, seeing the prophet's stern face, he sobers up.)* Prophet, you mean they deceived our ancestors with toffees, like what my mother sells, or this toffee is also proverbial, one of the teachings from your last seminar? *(He bows his head.)* Pray for me, Prophet.

Prophet: *(Ignores all the comments.)* So, you said you spied on her?

Ayeku: Prophet, you know, delicious soup draws a seat, sir! I only spied on her; I couldn't wait to be invited, sir. I have a plan for her, sir *(he started smiling, moved closer to the prophet, and whispered).* I'm not eager to court her right now. Nobody rushes to consume spicy pepper soup; maintaining a slow, steady pace as you lick the hot pepper soup can help you consume it successfully. You understand, sir?

Prophet: *(Shaking his head.)* Another sacrilegious and blasphemous statement. What has possessed you today? You're still referring to me by the name of "He whose name is a taboo." The leopard and the cheetah may look alike, but the leopard is a leopard, and the cheetah is a cheetah. I'm not, sir. I wear a cassock just like they did, but I'm not one of them. *(Angry)* Look, you fornicated with the lady; that's all.

Ayeku: No, I did not, sir. Sorry Prophet.

Prophet: You dare challenge the authenticity of the holy prophet's vision? What causes a sheep to bleat loudly is something the goat has already seen. What I see when seated, your eyes will not be able to see even when you climb the tallest coconut tree at Tofekope.

You dare challenge my vision. Have you heard about the new commandment I brought from the seminary? *(He paused.)* Why am I even asking when the house of Livingston is now your place of abode? *(He continues.)* Anyway, the new commandment that says that anyone who looks at a lady with a lustful eye other than me has fornicated with her?

Ayeku: I had no idea about this holy one. Does that mean if I look at her with a lustful eye, she is going to fall in love with me? *(He turns away from the prophet and murmurs.)* She's as hot as the midday sun. *(He raises his voice.)* If I had known that looking at her lustfully was a sin, I would have completed the sin by...

Prophet: By what? Look at your small mind again! A child eats a morsel of "fufu" according to the size of his mouth. Ahh, no wonder our elders say, "A crab does not beget a bird." You are just like your father, who would like to have a horizontal relationship with anything with a twin mound protruding from the chest. Behaving like a he-goat.

Ayeku: But prophet, you always said I'd be the one to take over after your demise. And that I'm not like the people in my cottage.

Prophet: Yes, you were good until now; ever since Livingston surfaced in this town, your attitude has been frivolous. Let me tell you a parable. You see, a man planted a seed in his vineyard and called the elders of the land to bless it so that it might not only grow beautifully but taste sweet as well. Are you with me?

Ayeku: Yes, Prophet. I guess that seed will be mango.

Prophet: I have decided not to respond to the devil speaking through you. As the seed germinated and the plant began to grow, nobody took notice of it until it began to mature; then passersby began admiring it with plans to have it in their backyard one day. Chiefs, fetish priests, teachers, and their servants observed her with wide, lustful eyes and gave compliments.

Ayeku: What kind of plant would the Prophet like to have in his backyard?

Prophet: I have vowed a vow not to succumb to the devil inside of you. Hmmm! Let me continue. The plant produced lovely blossoms and luscious, delectable fruits, but it also turned into a tripping hazard for men whenever they came into contact with it. They did not only admire its beauty; this time, gluttonously and lustfully, they desired to have it for themselves. But how on earth will the head sit for the knee to put on a cap? Isn't it proper, according to our custom and tradition, to have the local elders bless the festive food before it is consumed?

Ayeku: Did you also bring this from the seminary? And why was only one seed planted? Why are you speaking in parables?

Prophet: A wise child is spoken to in proverbs, not in plain language. As usual, when the fool is told a proverb, its meaning has to be explained to him.

While the prophet was counselling Ayeku, Mensa was also engaged in a similar conversation with Livingston. Livingston's residence was formerly the old adult education classroom block that the late doctor and some of the residents of the town constructed to improve the level of literacy in the town. It used to be a modest structure with collapsing mud walls and leaky thatched roofs packed with rickety benches. The structure, however, has changed from what it once was; it now benefits from thoughtful design and an abundance of light and air. Its floor now has floor-to-ceiling windows that open onto the beautifully landscaped courtyard, converting the living room into a virtual terrace so that one can have a similar light-filled living space and beautiful flooring, all thanks to the generosity of the town's youth, who renovated it to attract new teachers to the town. By using straightforward but exquisite décor, Livingston has been able to highlight the interior's attractiveness. He is sitting with Mensa in his beautiful hall.

Mensa: Sir, I care a lot about you, but are you not afraid of this daughter of Adam called Doeyo, whose drumbeats at odd hours of the day? *(He pauses.)* Hmmm! Let me tell you about this beautiful queen. It is said that there is a great mystery surrounding her birth, according to my grandmother, who was then serving as a "Trokosi" in the "Female Genital Mutilation House."

Livingston: What! Do you mean you practice Trokosi here?

Mensa: Yes, we do; it has been a long tradition with us, and not just Trokosi; we also practice female genital mutilation, and I hope it does not make us all devils. I guess you don't fully understand what Trokosi is. Hmm, I thought you knew everything. Okay, it is a system where children, especially young virgins, are made to atone for the crimes of their family.

Livingston: I know about that. It's all about young virgins and ritual servitude.

Mensa: Livingston, please speak English. I don't understand what you just said, but I thought you, of all people, were mature enough not to quickly judge other people's cultures. Anyway, that is not why I'm here; I'm here to inform... Furthermore, you recently taught us in social studies class that the best way to accept and understand other people's cultures is to first recognise our own cultural preferences, then respect those of others, and then attempt to reconcile, realise, and map the process, or that was for only us. I hope you are not ethnocentric. Livingston

Livingston: *(Cuts in.)* Okay, okay, go on, Mensa! You have been doing a lot of reading these days.

Mensa: As I was saying, my grandmother, who was then serving as a "Trokosi," claimed that Doeyo's mother, then one of the most stunning women in this town, was the only one who was unable to birth him a child after marrying the richest man in this town with many wives.

Livingston: And where from Doeyo, then?

Mensa: Why don't you give me a chance to finish, sir?

Livingston: Go on...

Mensa: Don't interrupt again, please. My grandmother claimed that Doeyo's mother had been childless for three years after her marriage, which had upset her in-laws and made her the target of ridicule throughout the town. In despair, she consulted the most powerful fetish priest in Tofekope to see if she could become a mother. She allegedly underwent one of the most gruesome rituals I've ever heard of, and on the final day, she was reportedly required to "go in between the sheets" with the fetish priest before receiving the promise of a child.

Livingston: That is really a horrible ritual! This was savagery!

Mensa: *(Moving closer.)* It's for your ears only, I am telling your ears, not your mouth. According to some rumours, it was later realised by the town doctor that there was nothing wrong with Doeyo's mother but rather that the other wives had been "reasonably unfaithful."

Livingston: *(Raising his voice.)* What? Was he impotent? And whose father is Doeyo, then? Is what I am assuming right?

Mensa: Your assumption is accurate, but I'm not going to say anything again if you keep interjecting, and please stop shouting. *(He moves closer and whispers in his ear.)* I was told that the doctor who requested a paternity test for Doeyo died within the week that the rumour broke out. However, the natives were of the opinion that Doeyo's mother went through that period of barrenness because she insisted on being married as prescribed by "He whose name is a taboo" before moving to her husband's house and also because she refused to undergo female genital mutilation.

Livingston: Did you believe it?

Mensa: That was the diagnosis of the priest. In any case, the entire community believed that. *(He lowers his voice.)* Again, the fetish priest had instructed Doeyo's mother not to do a number of things to the child, and should she break any of these prohibitions, calamity would strike this town.

Livingston: And did the mother go against any of the rules? What happened?

Mensa: Patience is the mother of a beautiful child. It appears that you have been possessed by an impatient spirit, as my mother would say. I was told, "oh, according to the fetish priest, the child was not to step into a church or hold a Bible; the next thing was that she was to marry the successor of the priest.

Livingston: Holy angels! If what I am assuming is right, won't that amount to incest? Anyway, did she go against the first one?

Mensa: Hmmm, wild cart as she was, I heard that when she chose to send Doeyo to the church for baptism by the late Prophet, she almost enabled the calamity prophesied to strike the community. The late prophet wasn't like this current prophet; he was a man I wish you had met. I was told that a sudden cloud formation occurred as the Prophet was holding her, and within a split second, the entire town was flash flooded. It was impossible to see the shorelines because of the extreme flooding.

Livingston: Did you believe this?

Mensa: That's what I've been told.

Livingston: And do you believe it?

Mensa: Why not? When a child has a strong mouth, he uses it to blow a horn, not a mortar gun. Anyway, I had no option but to believe. Howeverwhen I heard you teach the other day on the causes of rainfall, I thought it could demystify the notion that the flash flood was caused by the gods. Also, because you are close to Doeyo and you are also called sir, like the late town doctor, I decided to advise you to desist from this behaviour or you'll fall into the hands of that Trokosi and Female Genital Mutilation-infected house.

Livingston: *(Smiling.)* Thank you for caring about me.

Mensa: Before I forget, I also heard that on the day of her birth, there was a powerful whirlwind from the sea that was revolving so fast that it swept away everything in its path. Strangely, the wind devastated more than fifty homes before ending violently with the severing of Doeyo's umbilical cord. *(Just after saying this, Mensa leaves.)*

Livingston mulls over the Trokosi and Female Genital Mutilation issues. He remembers reading from one of the health journals that Trokosi is a practice that means "slave of a fetish." It demands that parents make their virgin girls available to fetish shrines as sex slaves in restitution or atonement for previous transgressions by family members. The rights and fundamental necessities of the victims are denied, along with physical and emotional maltreatment. But if this is horrible, female genital mutilation is worse. The term "female genital mutilation" he had learned while in school refers to a cultural practice in which the female sexual organs are damaged or the outer female private parts are partially or completely removed. In addition to being denied the opportunity to enjoy their sexuality, young girls who are made to undergo this procedure do so for cultural reasons and often have their rights cut, hacked, punctured, and ultimately burned. He paraphrased in his mind.

SCENE 4
The Weekly Durbar

It is the second day of the week, and, as usual, the drumbeat is audible from the big Odum tree. The evening is still young and romantic, and the townsfolk are all trooping and swarming in the direction of the sound. The moonlight exquisitely illuminated the entire town as the stars twinkled and glittered above, their light reflected by the sea and enhancing the romantic ambiance of the evening. The adolescents are in each other's arms, celebrating their newfound love under the moonlight as they stroll towards the venue. In contrast, the elderly men can be seen in groups in front, with their spouses following them in the company of their grandchildren.

Under the big odum tree, the drummers and dancers admirably portray how a despised fetish priest becomes famous in a town. The character of Wados, the fetish priest, is played by Doeyo. On Wados's way to the market, she happens to bump into a secret of the town. The chief of the town is dead, and the council of elders had met to choose three animals to be secretly sacrificed during the funeral of the chief. As a tradition, a contest will be held among the fetish priests in the town, and the priest who is able to identify the animals to be used is specially honoured. Wados came across some children playing in front of the chief's court and, pretending not to know what was going on, asked the children what was happening in the chief's court. The impenitent children innocently give her every detail of the ritual going on because of their disdain for her.

The whole place comes alive at this stage. There is screaming and shouting from the audience. Just then, the drumming abruptly stops, and the place becomes quiet as the chief's entourage and Livingston walk in. At that instant, Doeyo signals her group, and they all bow to acknowledge the presence of the elders. The drumming starts again, with the audience applauding and jubilating with the people on stage. In the play, a young man then came on stage to announce that it was the day of the contest. All the fetish priests in the town assemble and dance skillfully in turn as they give their answers.

However, none were able to answer the question correctly. When it came to the turn of Wados's master, the audience applauded and started jubilating. Wados's master, upon seeing this, decided to give her her best dance! She danced and danced to the admiration of the whole town until she forgot the answer to the question. At that instant, she stopped dancing, the whole place became quiet, and some in the audience started raining insults on her. Not knowing what to do, she gave out a loud noise and signalled to Wados about the situation.

Pretending to be possessed by a strange spirit, Wados jumped to the scene and began dancing erratically, gaining the full attention of her audience. Everyone was watching in full anticipation of what would come next. She skillfully danced her way to the priest, moving slowly and agilely, and as if biting his ear, she whispered to her master. Suddenly, the master gave out a loud noise and started jumping (but the other priests seemed angered by this) until her master stood still in front of the council and delivered the answer. At this stage, the audience ran onto the stage and carried Wados and her master on their shoulders, and they jubilated.

The noise dies down, and everyone is about to go home happily when an announcement comes from Doeyo that the group would like to perform another play for Livingston. At this announcement, the teacher's face registers surprise; the face of the chief gets contorted; and the fetish priest and Ayeku's faces go out of shape. The drumming starts again, but this time more romantic and in tune with the environment. They dance to the beat of the drums, portraying a man who is in love with a lady but is too shy to approach her and tell her. He adopts the persona of a covert lover who gives her lover gifts. Unfortunately, on the day he finally had the courage to confess his feelings to her, he was so overcome with joy that he tripped just a foot away from his secret lover, falling into her arms, but unluckily, in the process, he was pierced in the stomach by an old-rusted metal pole that was once a light pole on the beach but is now used to drag canoes. All he could say to her covert lover was, I love you, and the covert responded, I have also always loved you. The atmosphere changes; the whole place is quiet, with the young men yanking their wives and concubines to their sides and making sure they are breathing.

At this stage, Doeyo and her group bow to signal the end of the drama and wish the audience a good night. The audience claps to the drumbeat and starts heading home. The chief's face became as unsettled as a rain cloud, confused; the prophet was furious and perplexed, infuriated that there wasn't any kind of censorship since the scene was adult-oriented and again not scriptural; the priest and his entourage were in the woods, and no one could discern what they had just seen; it was a deviation and complete departure from the custom and tradition of the town. Teacher Ako is more bewildered and puzzled since he has never read any such story before. With all the men confused, Ayeku was lost at sea.

Some hours later, the teacher and Doeyo can be seen seated on a gravestone; the prophet is approaching.

Livingston: I am yet to witness such exceptional choreography in this town as that. You and your team are incredibly talented young women.

Doeyo: Thank you very much, sir. I do appreciate it. Anyway, sir, I have a problem I would like to discuss with you.

Livingston: You must be joking. How can a talented lady like you have a problem? (*He laughs.*) Ha ha, I'm just pulling your leg.

(By this time, the prophet is standing almost beside them; he interrupts the conversation.)

Prophet: I know that such filthy, fallacious falsehood could only come from a teacher who prepares his lesson notes on a gravestone with one of his pupils of the opposite sex at such an ungodly hour. What do you think you are doing with the lesson notebook in your hand? I assumed Teacher Ako was exaggerating when he told me about you.

Livingston: What did he say, sir? *(He rises from the tombstone.)*

Prophet: *(He ignores him and turns towards Doeyo.)* My daughter, what are you doing here at this ungodly hour with a man who prefers to be called by the name of "He whose name is a taboo?"

Doeyo: Prophet, I apologise if I sound rude, but I believe you were eavesdropping on our conversation.

Prophet: What? *(Gently shuffling and shoving Doeyo aside.)* No, I was just walking from Mama KK's place, after watching that slur you put up under the most revered place of our ancestors (looking Doeyo in the eyes), have you not been told that no man can outwit his ancestors? My dear, don't you think these jokes with this small boy have gone too far, or is it the education that has gone into your head? You know, if it hadn't been for me, you wouldn't have gotten this far in your education. You know how I have championed girl-child education in this town and how you, in particular, have benefited from that.

Livingston: But! (Moves close to the prophet.)

Prophet: *(Ignores him again and pulls Doeyo away.)* But what? My daughter, don't you know you are the only lady who has gotten to this level of education in this town? And all because I care so much about you, yet you think so little of me in this town and more about this small boy.

Doeyo: (Dumbfounded) But...

Prophet: Perhaps I'm only now beginning to realise. *(He pauses.)* But, my lady, do you not know that it is only the one who trims the family treasure who deserves to use it?

Livingston: But I was just... *(scratching his head)*

Prophet: Just what? The moment I saw you, I knew you would spark trouble, and when you started teaching, I knew it was the second time I would be denied this privilege. Young man, it is the woman whose child has been devoured by the witch who best knows the evils of witchcraft. If you were a member of my church, for your penance you would have rolled on the beach until rivers of water started to flow from your nose.

Doeyo: So, you were listening to our conversations, but my lord, he has said nothing bad apart from congratulating me for the performance under the big Odum tree, which you said was sacrilegious.

Prophet: Why won't he congratulate you? As I was saying, I was on an errand when I heard his blasphemous remarks. Well, I didn't want to listen to it, but I couldn't help hearing his remarks *(he again pulls Doeyo to his side)*. My daughter, I will advise you to keep your clothes on anytime you are in the company of this angel of darkness.

Livingston: *(Very unhappy.)* But, how can you say such a thing about me, sir? I could be your son.

Prophet: You are right; you could be my son, but you are not my son. My son would have understood that his work is to break the shell of a snail but not that of a tortoise. Because you are filled with pride and ambition, you have no room for wisdom.

Doeyo: But mighty one, you should know I'm not like that. And I don't engage myself in "horizontal relationships." And he is no angel of darkness.

Prophet: Remember, my lady, that while the salmon is no stranger to the salty sea, the tilapia is. As a prophet, what I see when seated, you cannot see, not even when you climb to the top of the coconut trees by the sea. *(Turning to the teacher.)* And you, don't you know that a child may have as many clothes as his father but not as many rags as the father? Or don't you know that just holding the Bible calculatedly fixed on my heart for two years gives me two spiritual years ahead of you? You've been crowned chief, but you're still working on your lucky charm. Do you want to be a god?

(They all depart in different directions, the teacher boiling in anger.)

SCENE 5
Mission House Consultations

A deep whistling is heard outside the walls of the church; an elderly man dressed in an old baby brown political suit with a large matching belt and "Achimota sandals" with long socks, making him look like an old colonial soldier, appears up the stairs to the front door of the mission house. Before he could knock, the prophet opened the door to welcome him.

Prophet: *(He extends his hand.)* Hello, Teacher Ako, you are most welcome to my humble abode. Come on in. Come on in.

Teacher: *(He walks into the modest but well-designed room with a lot of Christian artefacts.)* You call this a humble abode? Anyway, thanks for your hospitality. In fact, you've made my day with your smile.

Prophet: Don't be ridiculous. Anyway, how has your day been so far? Would you care for some water?

Teacher: I think I'm okay. I just had a calabash of palm wine from Mama KK's shed.

Prophet: I don't think you are trying to say that the palm wine quenched your thirst. Even if that is the case, you are not supposed to deny the living water of the Holy One.

Teacher: Okay, okay, I will take it for courtesy's sake.

Prophet: Thank you for that *(he brings him the water, and they sit down to talk)*. Anyway, you look down and worried, so if I'm not being nosy *(smiles)*, I'd like to know what's eating you up. Even if I am bothering you, it is part of my duty to pray about what distresses the souls of my sheep.

Teacher: You are right; your eye does not only see the human face but also penetrates the heart of the human soul, and that is very gracious of you.

Prophet: You've spoken highly of me, my brother, but you've not told me what seems so heavy on your mind. *(The school bell rings in the distance.)*

Teacher: The bell signifies a change of lesson, and I have a class to teach; I have to leave and come back later. What is happening to me is divine *(he looks up for a while, then says)*, and I have to save a soul before it perishes.

Prophet: When did you start saving souls, Teacher Ako? Have you become a missionary? Let

Teacher: *(His face changes.)* I don't think you can save this soul. I mean, not this one. This one is beyond your calling, my brother. You see, I have been dreaming lately.

Prophet: You don't mean you weren't dreaming previously.

Teacher: Oh, I did, but this is different. This is a God-given vision to save, and I have a "charge to keep." I have a "dying soul to save."

Prophet: You have a dream—a vision to save! Which is which? You mean you've been dreaming of saving someone? (Shocked) Who and from what? Who needs to be saved? And tell me, what do you dream about?

Teacher: *(He looks up.)* I think it is time.

Prophet: Time for what? Do you mind telling me, or will you continue to keep me in suspense? Besides, perhaps the Lord has revealed it to me as well.

Teacher: *(He smiles.)* Let me ask you a question. Do you think there is a need for the chief to marry again? I think he has had enough and should allow others to also marry the maidens in this town.

Prophet: Is that the dream? Ho! Do you mean you dreamed the chief had married enough? Anyway, who were you about to save in your dream?

Teacher: But don't you think the chief has married enough women? And the fetish priest as well.

Prophet: *(His smile fades away.)* Look here; in the first place, you came pulling my legs. You've expressed an opinion, and you expect me to comment on it. What is wrong with you? What about you? Have you not married enough too? Aren't you also involved in what you're religiously accusing them of?

Just then, there is a knock on the door, it was the town crier. The prophet goes over and sees the town crier.

Prophet: Come on in, oh, come in.

Town Crier: Thank you very much, Mighty One *(taking a few steps and stopping).*

Prophet: *(Looking at him in a strange manner)* For what?

Town Crier: *(Feeling quite uneasy)* Prophet, I'm fine. I'm not from the blue kiosk, and I'm not drunk. I'm on an errand for the chief.

Prophet: But town crier! Okay, go on *(he starts laughing).*

Town Crier: The chief said I should inform you that he would like to come and see you tonight for an important discussion.

Prophet: But town crier, I didn't say anything about you being drunk, or did I? Okay, tell the chief I will be expecting him. I will be at his service. Is that all? *(He is still looking at him strangely.)*

Town Crier: Mighty one, I think that's all. If there is any other business, I would like to come on my own to discuss it with you at a later date, but for now, I think that's all.

Prophet: Then have a nice day, and may God prevent you from getting even a glass of water from the blue kiosk. Look at the way you are walking like water at the bottom of a canoe, going from side to side, and yet you say you are not drunk. Oh, I've not said anything.

Town Crier: Thank you very much, Holy One. I will be on my way if there is nothing I can do for you.

Prophet: Anyway, before you leave, you know you owe me much rolling and romping on the beach in atonement for your inordinate choices. For your information, the number has increased exponentially.

Town Crier: Since when?

Prophet: Nonsense. If you can walk, you can dance, and if you can dance, you can roll on the beach.

Town crier: *(Giggles)* But prophet, as a town crier for this prosperous community, it is my obligation, duty, and privilege to taste all drinks used at the chief's court, be they good or bad. And miraculously, you don't expect me not to get drunk? That would go against the order of nature.

Prophet: That is not an excuse, my son; your righteous justification will not help. Do you know the verse in the Bible? Hmmm... but why should I ask you such a question when you spend your entire Sunday in the blue kiosk chatting with the old major glass?

Town Crier: Please, please, I don't want to sound disrespectful, but you don't mean I should vacate my post. My role in this community is a dignified one, sanctioned by the gods.

Prophet: I will not say that, nor will I request that you drink. I will not dignify your statement with a comment. As for your dignified role, we will discuss that later. *(He remembers that the teacher is waiting for him.)* Okay, Town Crier, I think I will have to attend to my visitor. I hope we can continue the conversation another time.

The prophet hurriedly walked into the room to continue the conversation with the teacher.

Prophet: *(He turns to the teacher.)* I do apologise for keeping you here for such a long time. I hope you still have some time to spend.

Teacher: Who was she, if I may inquire, and why did you spend too much time with her, or was she one of your…

Prophet: (He sharply cuts in.) Who said it's a she and one of my what? You have a big problem.

(Just then, there is another knock on the door, and Ayeku enters.)

Prophet: Do you need me, Ayeku?

Ayeku: No, Mighty One, I came to notify teacher Ako that we are with assembly.

Teacher: You are not "with assembly," you are at assembly, foolish boy. Inform our new teacher, Livingston, to close the school.

Prophet: Is Doeyo still in school? *(Before he answers)* I hope you have not forgotten your work in the church.

Ayeku: She is in; she is even leading the assembly. I will try to remember to come and perform my duties in the church. *(Ayeku smiles and leaves.)*

Prophet: I would like to apologise again. I'm very interested in what we were discussing, and will you go straight to the point with no circumlocution?

Teacher: Who came in earlier to see you? I am also interested in that.

Prophet: It was the town crier. Would you go on with your dream now?

Teacher: *(He gets up and goes around the chair on which he was sitting.)* My sentiments exactly! That was how it all started. The vision…

Prophet: I thought we were talking about dreams, not visions.

Teacher: Dreams and visions, visions and dreams. According to my dictionary, the two words almost mean the same thing. Visions, can be dreams, and dreams can be visions depending on where you are coming from.

Prophet: It's almost the same. So which one are you talking about, dreams or visions? *(He peeps into the inner chamber, sees his food has gone cold, and though angry with Teacher Ako's game, manages to keep his cool.)* Will you tell me about the dream, or should I go back to my priestly duties? *(Murmurs)* I'm not like you, who can leave your duties and pursue strange dreams.

Teacher: What did you say, please? Okay, I will tell you. In my dream, there was this beautiful bird. But before that, do you really think the chief should marry again?

Prophet: Would you please go on with your vision, or should I go back to my priestly duties?

Teacher: Okay, in my dream, I saw a very colourful bird perched on a large old Odum tree. I was overwhelmed by its beauty, to the extent that I had my eyes fixed on it for the rest of the day.

Prophet: I guess that day was not a holiday, and your pupils were in school waiting for you to attend to the duties for which you are paid.

Teacher: Yes, I said I would give up everything because of this bird. As I was saying, then something unfortunate happened.

Prophet: This is really regrettable. Why do you waste your energy on such frivolous activities when you are being paid to teach the pupils?

Teacher: Haven't you read about what happened to Abraham when God called him? I thought you should know better. Anyway, as I was saying, my gaze was still focused on the bird when I saw three powerful prey gliding through the air and descending in an uncompromising mood, all aimed at this little colourful bird. They came down in turns; the first to come down was the crow. As holy as it looked, it came in selfishly and greedily, with the intention of abusing the small bird. "Thus, sayeth the Lord" is the modus operandi of the crow with its long cassock. Just like Satan in the Bible, it was quoting the scriptures out of context. However, I managed to withstand its might, and I drove it away with that special anointing upon my life. *(He murmurs something.)* God is good. What made me angry was when he said,

"Touch not the Lord's anointed, and do my prophets no harm."

Prophet: You mean a special anointing? For teaching or healing?

Teacher: *(Ignores his comment.)* Then came the next prey, the vulture, notoriously lethargic and lazy, always using custom and tradition to its advantage. This bird preys on our ancestors and the deceased to defraud and deplete our meagre resources. Always takes what is rightfully due to others in the name of the gods. *(He pauses and asks a rhetorical question.)* Is it not strange that the vulture is behind every culture that is backward in its community? It also tried to abuse the little thing again, but I managed to fight it off.

Prophet: *(Asks sarcastically)* So, where was the vulture quoting from?

Teacher: Where else but customs and tradition?

Prophet: Please continue with your vision.

Teacher: As I was saying before, you rudely interrupted. The eagle, the ruler of the sky, with the wind under its control, was the last of the three birds to come around, and it was more powerful than the first two. The eagle was supposed to have vision, possess vitality, be fearless and tenacious, and, above all, not rely on dead customs. But this particular one was very, very foolish, always behaving like a puppet in the hands of the vulture and the crow. But I ward off the folly of the eagle, for what good is a stick when I've already swallowed the gong? What the eagle failed to realise was that a tree will always dance to the rhythm of the wind, no matter how great and strong it may be. Dealing with the eagle was very simple because I had already dealt with his two lieutenants, who were also competing for the same bird. When I thought the battle was over, from nowhere came a sparrow, also with the aim of disturbing the bird. This time, I did hit it so hard that I guess it will never look in the direction of this particular bird again. After this warfare, I stood under the tree and then heard this still small voice saying, "Victorious one," "man of valour." the Gideon of our time, take this bird. I have empowered you to save and protect it because you have fought a good fight. You have won the fight and taken the crown. Do you understand? Do you get the revelation?

Prophet: (*He bursts into uncontrollable laughter.*) The bird was saved by you, then. Teacher, teacher, little minds, don't put yourself through this. When the foolish man realises wisdom, know that he has exhausted all he has. Before you started, I knew what you were about to say, whether you called it a vision or a dream. What you are trying to say is that there is this lady you have to marry in order to save her from danger. Outstanding vision, or did you say dream?

Teacher: I thought you'd never get the revelation. How did you get it? I think you should add Joseph to your name.

Prophet: Before you started, I told you I knew where you were going to end; I guess the bird is Doeyo.

Teacher: Blessed are you among men, and blessed is the wisdom of your God. I'm sure God has revealed to you the work I am about to undertake. Thank God for today. He has revealed to his servant the good works he has appointed me to embark on.

Prophet: I presume the mighty prey includes the chief, the fetish priest, and myself. The sparrow happens to be Ayeku.

Teacher: I think you should add Daniel to your name as well. You have a spirit of discernment.

Prophet: If I'm one of the contenders, then why do you come to me?

Teacher: It's because you are a man of God, and you will understand me better than any of them. Besides, men of God are obligated to marry only one. *(He turns away from him.)* Thank God for revealing it to you. Thank God, I don't have to include the man of God in the warfare.

Prophet: Nobody revealed anything to me. It is written all over your face. Besides, if there is any mighty prey or greedy bird, I think you are the one since you already have ten wives and more concubines, but for the fetish priest. Remember, when a man with many wives falls ill, he starves to death.

Teacher: What are you saying, Prophet? I'm not a palm tree to be self-sufficient; even the dead want an increase in their number; how much more the living? You are obligated to marry one, and I think it goes with the privileges you enjoy. All of these are advantages.

Prophet: Okay, teacher, I appreciate you reminding me of my responsibilities, but! Hmm.

Teacher: Thank you very much for your understanding. At the end of the dream, I married the bird, and we lived happily ever after, just like the story I have been reading to the children at school.

Prophet: You mean Doeyo.

Teacher: Yes, you may say that.

Prophet: Don't you think you would be carrying a tortoise home, thinking you had made a good catch? And what about the new bird that just arrived?

Teacher: You mean Livingston? I will ask the education unit to recall him if he tries anything foolish.

Prophet: You are still confused.

SCENE 6

At the Chief's Court

Discussing the Delicacy of the gods

While the teacher is talking to the prophet about Doeyo, the fetish priest has also gone in to see the chief on the same issue.

Priest: Greetings, mouthpiece of the living. The gods send their blessings and regards.

Chief: Welcome, mouthpiece of the gods. Why do you have to wait by the door when you are about to enter your own home? Anyway, everybody is fine here. The gods have been good to us these days. There is always a bumper harvest. I have just finished settling the disputes between Papa Doe and Mama Yaa, so you see, everything is fine here.

Priest: The gods must be praised. I'm a very fine ruler of the living, and everything is fine with the family. We are all fine; the gods are really showering their blessings on us.

Chief: Would you mind if I sent for the linguist?

Priest: Is that necessary? In any case, I don't mind, but since he is not here, I guess we can proceed. Besides, what I'm about to discuss with you does not need the presence of your linguist, if the ruler of the living does not mind.

Chief: *(Not liking the idea since the priest always seemed to have his way anytime the two met to discuss important issues.)* I think we can go on, but first, I do not appreciate the arrogance of the people of Mukope these days *(he signals the servant to serve some drinks)*. Even though the people of Mukope know they are our slaves, they are beginning to misbehave, according to complaints by my elders. Now the elders are reminding me that there can be no kingdom without rules, and that is what the people in Mukope need.

Priest: *(Very eager to contribute)* Yes, yes; it is one of the things I came to discuss with you. If we continue on the path of leniency, we will be destined for destruction.

Chief: Yes, it's been quite a headache for me, but the linguist seems to be at home with it, so I guess I don't have to worry about it. *(He forces a smile.)* In any case, you can continue with what you came to discuss.

Priest: Ruler of the living, you know calamity befalls anyone who tries to undermine the wisdom of the gods, and I guess the calamity that almost befell this town when Doeyo's mother angered the gods is still fresh in our minds. Remember what happened when the town crier refused to accept the ruling of the gods? Remember...

Chief: *(Cuts in very fast.)* Mouthpiece of the gods, wait, is any calamity about to befall this town? Are the gods already brewing calamity for this town?

Priest: *(Happy about the direction of the conversation.)* Calamity will be an understatement. They've almost started brewing a catastrophe of enormous proportions, but you know they always reveal it to me before they act.

Chief: Don't you think this has more to do with taking too much alcohol in the evenings before going to bed than the signs from the gods? *(Annoyed)* And what has led to the brewing of this pot of calamity? We've enjoyed tranquilly for some time now, even when the new teacher, Livingston, asked us not to slaughter any animals anytime it rains because rains involve a natural cycle instead of the work of the gods. I think he was making a lot of sense when he spoke to the council of elders. I wonder what the gods want now.

Priest: *(Ignoring the remarks)* Ruler of the living, you know, that young man can't teach us our traditions and customs. According to the powerful oracles of the great house of Tofekope, Doeyo is to marry the successor

of the great fetish priest and no other
person. However, it seems the living want
to fish in the ponds of the gods, and this is
dangerous. (He stands up.) You know, one
does not rub himself in oil and lie by the
fire to sleep.

Chief: Don't you think this is more personal indulgence
and gratification than the god's demand?
So then that means you are the one eligible
to marry Doeyo, right?

Priest: I think that it is the wish of the gods, and the
living cannot deny the gods their wish.
The edicts of the gods are the divine laws
of this land, and any other law found to
be inconsistent with any of these edicts
shall, to the extent of the inconsistency,
be null and void. And I am sure the ruler
understands these rules of engagement
with the gods.

Chief: In this case, can't any alteration be made so that
the ruler of the living can partake in the
delicacy of the gods?

Priest: The gods do not change their minds, and their
wishes must be carried out to the letter.

*Just then the linguist enters, babbling, startled when he
becomes aware of the presence of the chief and the priest.*

Linguist: Apologies for the interruption, mighty ones.
I was overtaken by the events of the day,

which clouded my vision and judgement. May I once again ask for forgiveness?

Priest: Your apology has been accepted *(he is not happy with the presence of the linguist)*.

Chief: Apologies accepted *(the chief is happy)*. By the way, linguist, if you don't mind, would you like to listen to the mouthpiece of the gods? According to him, there seems to be a calamity brewing for this town, and I think you have to hear this, or, what do you say, mouthpiece of the gods?

Priest: Oh, we... hmmm! I don't mind, since he also sits in council with the gods.

Linguist: *(Getting angry)* What calamity again? Aren't the gods asking too much from the living? At least they do nothing more than eat, sleep, hear cases, and receive messages. They should come and see how sweat runs down our bodies like the Volta River.

Priest: Be careful you don't fall into the wrath of the gods. Please exercise some decorum. A good tongue watches over the head because the tongue can inflict more wounds than a knife.

Linguist: What exactly is the issue? If it's about the people of Mukope, we have no problem, except that they refused to allow me, I mean me (beating his chest), to marry that slave daughter of theirs. If they don't comply, they'll have to...

Priest: I believe this is just the beginning, and as I've said, if we continue in our line of action, they will have us as their slaves, and history will just be repeating itself.

Linguist: Stop that priest! Even the gods themselves are not immune to fate. What line of action do you mean, mouthpiece of the gods?

Chief: *(Intervenes sarcastically)* According to the mouthpiece of the gods, he, and nobody else, is to marry Doeyo. If anybody attempts to do that, the whole town will taste the wrath of the gods.

Priest: *(He cuts in quickly.)* Hmm. Linguist, you are turning your mouth into a knife; it will one day cut off your lips. I am sure you are well aware of how the people of Mukope came to be our vassal state. This similar mindset exhibited by Mukope's leaders led to the town fighting useless battles, which they ultimately lost and are now our vassal state. It was told later that the whole situation was brewed by the gods to punish the people of Mukope. You seem to be closing your eyes to facts, and unfortunately, the only avenue to learn would be through accident.

Linguist: What makes him the sole individual eligible to marry her? After all, we are all children of the gods. Besides, if anybody is more eligible to marry Doeyo, it should be you, chief, because you rule the living, and until the living are satisfied, the gods can't be fed. Or is it not the living that makes the inhabitants of the spirit world long for mashed yam, ahi?

Priest: Linguist, it is the same directive of the gods and customs that you are using to annex someone's wife, the young lady from Mukope. Why are you picking and choosing the directives of the gods? Again, I have warned you of your insubordination to the gods. The gods do not wait for the living before they eat their delicacies. Furthermore, they do not depend on the living for their sustenance.

Linguist: I'm not trying to be disrespectful to the gods; far from it, but I think they have to apprise themselves of current trends. Besides, these days, people without wings fly in the afternoon in metal cans, and the last time I visited the big city, I saw young men killing themselves to make a living. Also, we are no longer infants; we are all big children.

Chief: *(Annoyed)* Can't anyone stand in for Doeyo, or are you in love with the maiden? You know she can't stay in that Trokosi and female-genital-mutilation house. You, of all people, should know that the fish and the bird may fall in love, but the two cannot build a home.

Linguist: That's very true, and now that she has been taught in school the cause of rainfall and the reason why there are bumper harvests at certain times of the year, she will be a wild horse at the shrine; in fact, I believe she will end up converting all the ladies serving for the crimes of their families to Christianity. And, to be honest, you know those lovely young ladies shouldn't be languishing in that Trokosi and female-genital-mutilation house for crimes they never committed. So, let's have a win-win situation; let's substitute someone else for Doeyo.

Chief: What did the young man even say about the cause of the rain? You don't know, do you, mouthpiece of the gods?

Linguist: *(Scratching the head)* The water cycle might be one. Yes, yes, water cycle; my children were saying it the other day. In fact, they managed to persuade me better than you did the other time, mouthpiece of the gods. That was why the last sheep took a while to show up.

Priest: Are you two trying to say this small boy's assertion carries more weight than that of our ancestors? *(He laughs, then gets angry.)* Our ancestors might have been fallible, but their judgement should not be measured or compared with that of a drooling child; he is just a suckling child.

Chief: We know he is a suckling toddler, and we may not trust him, but you see, everything he says sounds convincing. Hence, it is difficult not to have faith in what he says, as compared to you, who only make demands without explanation. Besides, when a child learns to wash his hands well, he eats with the elders. Do you remember your father's explanation for the challenge my father had the last time when he decided to follow customs instead of wisdom by sitting on his scrotum for hours? That young man has corroborated the assertions of the late doctor again.

Priest: *(Cuts in angrily)* Every respected society is built on customs and traditions, and our customs and traditions have been the bedrock of this community, so what happened, mouthpiece of the living? He may sound convincing, but he is not right. He may sound like an expert, but spirituality has nothing to do with logic. It is through the guidance of our ancestors that we have learned to appreciate the past, understand the present, and have hope for the future. Why throw all that away and make such a detour because of a suckling toddler? Don't you think the boy is performing the same role as "He whose name is a taboo?"

Linguist: What we are saying is that you don't sound convincing, like he does. By just introducing insect repellant into this town, Livingston has managed to significantly lower the number of individuals who fall sick in this town, which has resulted in a decline in the daily flock of sheep waiting outside the gate of your house for atonement. He sounds more convincing, that is all.

Priest: *(He cuts in.)* "He whose name is a taboo" sounded convincing when they forced us to sell our gods and people to them. Even the prophet knows the evil one can come as an angel of light.

Linguist: We're not saying we don't see him as such. However, we think the gods are demanding too much nowadays. *(He turns to the priest and asks sarcastically.)* And what prevented our gods from defending themselves when they were being sold?

Priest: Linguist, I have warned you about the way you address the gods. The gods do not change their minds. Furthermore, I have said a number of times that it's not for personal gratification. I just came to inherit this custom. The gods have enshrined and established this decree. I just want to save this town, that is all. Again, these traditions that we talk about were passed on to me by our forefathers. Er, it's not my fault.

Linguist: Yes, we are aware our ancestors devolved these customs to us. But can the same be said if your head is at stake to save this town? Anyway, you should know that a priest who invokes a calamity on his people for personal gain must remember that he cannot prevent his house from being destroyed by the same calamity.

Priest: Linguist, I guess my family's reputation for integrity and bravery is not up for debate. You should use your wisdom to build bridges rather than erect dams and walls in times of calamity and crisis. *(Turned towards the chief)* My leader, a chief, has a peaceful reign when he receives sound counsel. I believed the counsel you're receiving to be contrary to what our elders advised.

Linguist: Oh no, I don't mean to imply that; it just sounds like a fortuitous and convenient coincidence. My reference is to you, not your family. The custom, you claim, was truly passed down to you by our ancestors, but who wouldn't be privileged to wage such a war if it hangs on the neck of one of the most stunning ladies in this town to wed him? Priest, you understand that this has nothing to do with courage and that professing grandeur won't make you great.

Chief: Priest, you did not answer my earlier question. What happens if I get the chance to marry the pretty lady myself? Are the gods still going to bestow calamity on us?

Priest: That's why I came here; once the gods make a decree or agree on a decision, the living cannot alter, amend, or change it. Amending or altering it will culminate in a calamity of greater proportions. *(He continued).* Do you recall?

Linguist: *(quickly retorts)* We recall everything, all the calamities. All we are saying is that the gods must adopt a modern approach to looking at things. We are living in a different era from the one they lived in, and they have to change their taste to suit our customs today. We are hard-pressed to meet their demands all the time. Today, newborn babies have had to go to school because grandparents are on the field working. Instead of enforcing who marries whom, the gods must recognise this and address our harvest.

Priest: I have cautioned you to be mindful of the way you talk about the gods. The spirit world has different rules.

Chief: *(interjects)* By the way, how many wives do you have? And how many of the Trokosi ladies do you intend to add to your wives?

Priest: I currently have fourteen, and, respectfully, I have not thought of adding any of the Trokosi yet.

Linguist: Priest! Don't you think it is morally time we looked into this Trokosi conundrum? Won't the gods be happy if they see these Trokosi ladies marrying some of the bachelors in this town? Why should the young men of the town move to the next town to marry just because of some old ritual? This whole Trokosi thing is morally ambiguous.

Priest: As I keep saying, linguist, you are a beneficiary of this custom, yet you fight it when this same custom bequeaths privileges to others. I came here worried about the calamity hanging over this town and how we could solve it, and all the two of you are doing is berate me for something I inherited.

Chief: *(The chief quickly assumes the role of a peacemaker.)* Anyway, thank you very much, mouthpiece of the gods. However, I would like to take this decision in consultation with the other elders, even on the Trokosi and the female genital mutilation. I believe that going forward, we all must learn to discuss such sensitive issues dispassionately for the good of our people.

Priest: Chief, this is an emergency, and there must be a sense of urgency. We are in a crisis, and you need not consult the elders about it. Doeyo should have married the shrine "yesterday."

Linguist: Priest, we don't stay on the yam farm and bargain for the price of the yam. He said he would consult his elders, and I think it concerns them as well if calamity is being brewed for this town by the gods. Besides, it is in the gods' best interests to accommodate our shortcomings; otherwise, I doubt there will be anyone to offer them mashed yams. But priest, don't worry about the people of Mukope. *(He turns to walk away.)* However, I think we must revisit this Trokosi issue.

Priest: I don't know what your problem is, Linquist. But it seems you don't understand what is happening. If you are attentive, you will hear the crabs coughing loudly.

Linguist: I know the crabs have the ability to cough. However, make sure you don't end up like the leopard that picks the tortoise home, only to end up starving to death.

The fetish priest is in an angry mood as he says goodbye.

Chief: What do you think about this, Linguist?

Linguist: I think the gods are demanding too much these days. If it is because of the people of Mukope, I have them under control. The fact that I want to marry the slave girl is purely my decision, and the gods should not intervene.

Chief: *(Very relaxed)* Tell me, Linguist, how many wives do you have?

Linguist: Only seven, chief.

Chief: Seven, and you think it is not enough. Have you also not had enough?

Linguist: Not as much as the fetish priest. At least you have fifteen wives. Mine is only half that of the priest, and besides, don't you think we should all be on par?

Chief: Anyway, I have to see the prophet for a very important discussion.

Later, when the chief is about to leave for the prophet's place, the messenger runs in to inform him that his nephew is at the door.

SCENE 7

At the Riverside

The pond is just a stone's throw away from the river, and Doeyo can be seen from afar carrying a gourd on her head with a bucket in her hand. In a few minutes, she comes into full view of the women washing, fetching water from the pond, and gossiping.

Mama Doe: *(laughing)* Hello, my neighbours. Have you heard the latest gossip in town? *(Long pause.)* Hmm! Men!

Mama Owe: You always have something new. What is it this time? You should have married either the town crier or the chief's messenger.

Mama Ogbo: Speak up! I would like to hear. No woman is safe as far as the species called man is concerned.

Mama Doe: It's about your husbands. That is why, after the fetish priest subjected me to all those abuses, I decided not to marry any of the men around me. Anyway, the source of the gossip is fresh from the palm wine seller's shed. The rumour is that your husbands are fighting over the young maiden coming to fetch water. *(She says this, pointing in the direction of Doeyo.)*

Mama Owe: Be careful, since you are talking about the most powerful men in this town who wield a lot of authority.

Mama Doe: Are they not men with married partners, or are you trying to say your husbands are now about to take the oath of celibacy after marrying a minimum of five with uncountable concubines, apart from the prophet?

Mama Sacketey: What is the source? My dear, these are heavy allegations.

Mama Doe: Do you expect me to tell you? If I'm mute and blind, does that make me smile, even when I know I am stepping into fire? I'm okay enough to know the people I'm gossiping with. There will soon be a civil war in this community because of this beautiful young maiden.

Mama Naa: When you say husbands, is mine included? He promised me that I would be his last wife. That is why I left my first love, Yaboh, for him.

Mama Ogbo: Why is your husband the head of the Vatican? What exempts him from it, or are you trying to say he is not the father of your children and you are not Mama Naa's rival?

Doeyo approaches them and greets them, to which they all respond enthusiastically.

Mama Doe: How are you, Doeyo, and how is the school doing so far?

Doeyo: I am doing well. Thanks for asking, and I am enjoying school; we are learning a lot of new things.

Mama Yaa: What about your young teacher? I hope he is also fine. *(They all look at Doeyo.)*

Doeyo: You mean Mr. Livingston? Oh, he is fine, and since his arrival, we are all thriving.

Mama Saa: What do you mean by that? *(boiling)* Hasn't my husband, Teacher Ako, been doing well before he came? Ungrateful people!

Mama Doe: Oh, Mama Saa, I think that is not what she is trying to say. Don't get her wrong. All she is trying to say is that she has been getting along well with the young man. That's all *(turns to Doeyo, smiling)*, or my sister, what do you say?

Mama Dey: I don't think that was what she said. Since that small-boy-big-man they called Livingston arrived, the entire town seems to attribute everything good to him. Eh, *(she straightens herself and pushes her clothes up)* eh! To the extent that his views are compared with those of the gods. The other time my husband went to...

Mama Yaa: *(Cutting in quickly)* Hei Hei! The issue is between your husband and the chief. All the chief said was that Livingston's explanation of the reason why rain falls during certain months of the year is more credible than that of your husband. The chief only said that your husband's explanation of why it rains in certain months of the year is less convincing than that of Livingston.

Mama Dey: I believe this is not the forum for such discussion, yet you have gone ahead to discuss it—such a taboo! sacrilege!

Mama Doe: What's taboo? Don't you think your husband and his family have held this town to ransom for too long? Even a mosquito bite on the chief needs the blood of a bull as a sacrifice. I believe the number of bulls sent to that house can build this town just the way "He whose name is a taboo" built the city.

Mama Yaa: Mama Doe, don't dabble in things you have no knowledge of oooh …

Mama Owe: She is telling the truth, in my opinion. Your husband has cashed in too much in this town. Do you recall the incident when the elderly chief unintentionally sat on his "valuable assets" during the case between Mama Ama and the town crier? Due to some ancient custom that states that once a chief sits, he must remain sitting unless he desires to excuse himself from the audience, he was unable to stand up and ended up in the hospital. The elderly man was forced to wait on his "valuable asset" until he was rushed to the hospital.

Mama Doe: *(Continues)* As if that wasn't enough, after spending all that money at the hospital, your husband, I mean the Priest, said that was the act of the gods and that the gods were angry.

Mama Yaa: I think this young teacher is carrying a truckload of problems. Wherever his name is mentioned, there seem to be problems. Wherever he is from, I am sure they swept his footprints after him with a broom the moment he left.

Doeyo: *(Defending)* It seems you people don't understand him. That is why you are all saying what you are saying about him. As to the issue of the rain, even I can explain it to you if you will all allow me to. However, it seems you have already formed your opinion about him, so...

Mama Yaa: So, we know you understand him. Even the wife of the executioner understands that it's the duty of her husband to behead people, not that the husband is evil, so we are not surprised. What do you say, ladies? After all, the owner of a smell will never notice it. I believe all of us would have behaved in a similar fashion if we were in her shoes.

(They are all quiet; Doeyo bids them goodbye.)

Mama Owe: Anyway, tell us the people involved in this race to win this pretty lady who understands everything, my dear.

Mama Doe: I said all the kingpins in this town. As to other people, I don't know, but if the flower is attractive, it attracts all kinds of butterflies.

Mama Key: What do you mean, all the kingpins?

Mama Doe: I mean exactly what I said. The priest, the prophet, your chief, the teacher, even your son, Ayeku.

Mama Yaa: That is a serious accusation; my husband is not interested in women.

Mama Doe: How many official wives does your husband have?

Mama Yaa: He has 14, but he loves me.

Mama Doe: Who is the last person he married?

Mama Yaa: Me.

Mama Doe: *(Counting on her fingers)* You got married about two years ago! He is now 45 years old. Count the year's interval. He betrothed his first wife at the age of fifteen, and you are his 14th wife. Mathematically, if I am correct, it means that every two years he gets married, right? It means your term will expire soon *(she starts laughing)*.

Mama Yaa: That would be very foolish of him; at least Doeyo is very young.

Mama Owe: You were as young as she is now when you got married.

Mama Naa: I have also heard the rumours.

(They are leaving; the town crier comes in, drunk.)

Town Crier: *(Tottering)* foolish women, always gossiping, you all refused to say, "I do," to me.

All: Marry who? With your tattered clothes? Go and marry the "old major" in the blue kiosk.

SCENE 8

Mission House
A Discourse between the Chief and the Priest

Greetings are heard outside the church as the chief enters the churchyard, clad in a beautiful adinkra cloth and matching sandals. He enters the mission house just as the prophet comes out of the inner house; they meet halfway between the pulpits.

Prophet: You are welcome.

Chief: Thank you, Prophet.

(After allowing the chief to sit down, they start talking.)

Prophet: You are welcome again, and I hope everything is fine with you. *(Beaming)* I am fine and just finished counselling some young ladies. I have been anticipating your visit ever since the town crier brought the message.

Chief: Thank you, Prophet. All is well with me. I think you can see that this town is flourishing all because of my ingenuity and your prayers, but I came to discuss a personal issue with you, not about this town. I hope your wife and concubines are all fine.

Prophet: Then, chief, you are welcome, and I'm ready for our discussions, but you know I have not added any other woman to my wife.

Chief: Forgive me, I instantly forget you are a prophet. The issue is quite simple and straightforward. You know, almost four festivals have passed since I got married, and during this next festival, I would like to take another wife.

Prophet: I think it is fine with me when you are ready; I will be there to bless the marriage when invited.

Chief: That is very nice of you; my ancestors won't forgive me if I forget about you. Ever since this town was established, the church has blessed the marriages of my forefathers, so I don't think it will be appropriate if you are not invited. After all, I wouldn't want to be the first to deviate from a well-established culture.

Prophet: Thank you so much for such a compliment to the church. The church will be there to support the chief on such a memorable occasion. It will be our privilege.

Chief: That is good news because rumours are rife and circulating in town that you are interested in the lady I will be marrying.

Prophet: *(Restrains himself from getting angry.)* God forbid, she is too young to marry, even to a chief, a priest, a teacher, or anybody else. Especially since we have all embraced girl-child education.

Chief: How do you know the lady in question? Is there any truth to the rumours going around? And are you saying the teacher is also proposing to marry her? Then I guess the rumours might be true. And what do you mean she is too young?

Prophet: I don't know about the rest. However, I think the little girl should not be forced into marriage by anybody, not even the new teacher or any of his pupils. Our girls should be allowed to grow and become like those in the city.

Chief: You don't mean the new teacher is also interested in Doeyo? What has come over the youth these days? Somebody should make them aware that when a child is learning a craft, he does not begin with the skin of a leopard.

Prophet: I didn't say he was.

Chief: That's better; otherwise, his head would have been on the altar of the gods. The fact that he is quite knowledgeable would have made it a perfect sacrifice for the gods. I hope you are on my side.

Prophet: Yes, oh yes, as long as you do the right thing. Anyway, there is something more important I would like to discuss. What is happening in Mukope?

Chief: Oh, those slaves; the linguist wants to marry one of them, which I even consider taboo, but the people of Mukope do not see the privilege of their daughter marrying the linguist. I think that has angered him. He increased their tolls, and now they are refusing to pay.

Prophet: But chief, I heard the lady at the centre of the dispute is married.

Chief: Oh yes, but the husband is at this moment in our dungeon waiting to be executed.

Prophet: Execution! For what offence? For loving a woman and marrying her? This is foolishness.

Chief: How do I know? The linguist can explain better. But maybe for eating in the same bowl with the elders.

Prophet: *(Very angry at this point.)* But you are the chief! I heard they got married before the linguist set his eyes on her. Sources also indicate that she is not interested in that stiff-neck idiot. Why can't you people be content with your wives? Why add more? And it's making you people very foolish.

Chief: I hope I didn't hear foolish. Anyway, the reason for adding another wife is simple: it shows how powerful we are. For the people of

Mukope, it's all about tradition—you know, once a slave, always a slave.

Prophet: But Chief, if it's tradition, then I think the priest should marry Doeyo.

Chief: You don't sound in favour of the linguist's decision. For now, I am more interested in my marriage than the head of the slave. You can discuss it with the linguist if you want.

Prophet: That fool? This is not acceptable.

Chief: Prophet, I think I would like to take leave of you. My nephew would like to discuss a matter with me.

Prophet: God bless you, mighty one, and I guess I don't need to wear my prophetic mantle to predict what he is going to discuss with you.

Ayeku is waiting at the chief's court. Supper has been served on the table; he starts salivating; the chief is late. Just as he swallows another drop of saliva, the chief enters.

Chief: Son, I'm sorry for the delay. I'm from the churchyard, and the prophet sends his greetings.

Ayeku: That's very kind of him.

Chief: Let's eat very fast so we can go to the durbar grounds and watch your colleagues perform.

Ayeku: I heard Doeyo will be performing this evening. Do you like her performance, Uncle? *(Before he can answer the question)* do you think she will make a good wife

Chief: *(Astonished)* I think we should be very fast and discuss your problems and other things. I am very interested in what is troubling you.

The chief and his nephew move to the courtyard after the sumptuous meal.

Ayeku: Thank you so much. The food is wonderful. It's been a very long time since I've eaten something like this. Uncle, I hope I will be invited at another time.

Chief: You are welcome, son. I think I am ready to hear about your problem.

Ayeku: Uncle, you see, hmm, I have a question.

Chief: You better ask, or else we will be late for the programme.

Ayeku: Uncle, how old were you when you married?

Chief: Why didn't you ask your father?

Ayeku: I mean, when you married Mama Vida, how old were you?

Chief: Not now, son. Will you get straight to the point? We are losing time, and I don't want to get there late. You know I am the chief and must lead by example.

Ayeku: I'm sorry. Can I? I mean, I'm not sure what to say, but can I? At my age?

Chief: Can you do what at your age? Don't be silly, boy; you can get married at any age. You are a man and a royal.

Ayeku: *(Smiling)*

Chief: When I got married, I was five years younger than you are now. Didn't your father tell you about my exploits? Get up, and let's move.

Ayeku: Thank you very much, uncle.

Chief: Why? Did your father say you couldn't marry? We are royals! Your veins are filled with the blood of royalty.

Ayeku: Oh, no.

Chief: I better go and change so we can get going; I can hear the thundering drums from here. *(He enters the chamber and returns very fast; Ayeku is still smiling.)*

SCENE 9
At Durbar Grounds
A Play of Hard Truths

The skies have been very cloudy both in the morning and in the evening. The moon's light dims as if it is being forced to shed its light. The drumbeats sound like a rolling dirge, sorrowing in line with the weather. When the light came on, an able-bodied man with fetish markings on his head, shoulders, and legs with hair in dredlocks appeared from nowhere, laughing and pulling banded ropes that he held in his hand. Suddenly, a burst of loud laughter made the hairs of the audience stand on end. There is a moment of silence, and the stage lights go off again. A portion of the light on stage reappears, and the man who appeared earlier can be seen pulling the ropes again, though what is tied to the rope cannot be seen. As the lights on the entire stage come alive, the man can be seen pulling women bound and tied to the ends of the ropes. The women are being dragged on the floor as they sing a soft dirge in anguish. Instantly, the audience gets a full view of what is happening on the stage. The drumming ceases, and only the soft, anguishing dirge of the women and the laughter of the man dragging them can be heard.

Doeyo suddenly appears dressed like one of the women. With tears all over her face, her voice rings out:

"*They say it is called Trokosi.*
An atonement (a sob)
They say it is called Trokosi.
Ritual servitude
They say it is called Trokosi.
Ritual servitude, where traditional religious shrines take young maidens as payment.
As religious atonement for the alleged misdeeds of a family member.
They call them Trokosi.
Wives of the gods: Which gods and where are they?
See, those with eyes to see
See how helpless these women are, being dragged on the floor.
Hear, those with ears to hear.
Hear their dirge as they are dragged helplessly across the floor.
How many of us would like to walk their walk?
How many of us will give up our own to suffer through this?
They are paying for a crime they have never committed.
A crime they might not even have heard of
how wicked and inhumane it looks and sounds
My heart weeps for these women.
The suffering, the torture, the brutalities
What they go through is just beyond description.
He laughs and rejoices over their pain and misfortune.
Oh, how cruel this world is.
That one is punished for a crime she did not commit.

It's true that life is not fair, but for how long will this go on?

How my heart wails for these women,

as they are locked up in the manacles of human sadism.

This must be stopped. It must be stopped. No more, no more..."

There is a loud sound of victory that can be heard from afar as Doeyo unties the ropes binding the Trokosi and frees them from the shackles of cruelty. Everyone in the crowd cheers, including the fetish priest, who could not read the meaning of the performance. The drums start, and there is dancing and merrymaking.

Suddenly, the fetish priest realises that his power base is under attack. He is beside himself with confusion; there is nothing he can do. He leaves the durbar grounds in fury and unconsciously goes past his own house.

SCENE 10
At the Shrine
A Game of Symantics

At the shrine, the Trokosi and other wives of the priest are discussing the drama they had watched under the Odum tree when the priest emerges angrily from his room. One Trokosi lady accosts him.

Trokosi: Priest, don't you think the drama was wonderful?

Another Trokosi: Yes, yes, it was a wonderful drama.

Priest: If it were your eyes that didn't see, are you telling me your minds were so clouded you could not discern the message they were trying to send across? I never knew I only had a horde of idiots under my roof.

Trokosi: We are sorry if we made you angry.

Priest: Get away from my face and call me Mama Sacketey.

(In a moment, his wife comes.)

Priest: Go to the prophet and inform him that I would like to discuss an important issue with him.

Mama Sacketey: You've never been to the churchyard since you were installed as the great priest of Tofekope. Why today? *(She is trying to see if she can guess the purpose of the visit by her husband.)* You can confide in me, or you don't trust me?

Priest: This is for men only. It's not an issue of trust; it's an emergency to save this town from the calamity the gods are brewing. Unless there is a timely intervention, this whole town will be lost.

Mama Sacketey: Why are the gods so demanding these days? I heard they are demanding you marry another woman. Are they not aware that the strength of a man deteriorates with age, or don't you tell them? But if they are all-seeing, do they see your performance these days?

Priest: *(Very furious)* What exactly should I tell them? You are really bold! You're so daring! Who have you been conversing with? You had better be careful, or you'll end up slaughtering a cow. Are you implying that I am no longer a man? Do you mean to suggest that I am only half a man? Have you ever bothered to interrogate the young women about my conjugal prowess?

Mama Sacketey: I have never said anything like that, and I don't expect you to put words in my mouth. All I was trying to say is that your energy seems to be dwindling with your age, and it seems to be catching up very fast with you these days. I recently heard a prophet remark that a person's strength increases as their days do, yet we all know that when it comes to conjugal duties with men, it is the reverse. Besides, you are not getting any younger, and there is nothing else to prove.

Priest: I hope you have not been gossiping about me. You better keep your mouth shut, or the gods will shut it for you.

Mama Sacketey: My husband, you know I have aged with these threats. When will you ever defend yourself? Every single conversation comes with the issuance of a threat from the gods. I'm no gossip. As a matter of fact, all I have been trying to say is that maidens are an endangered species nowadays, so you better be careful. Trying to prove that you are the true son of the Tofekope Shrine will put you in your grave. The truth hurts, but it's like ageing; the earlier you accept it, the better you will accept the looks that come with your age.

Priest: Woman, I called you to send you to the prophet, not for you to brief me on the state of my prowess when performing my conjugal duties. "Something must kill a man," and

I am all for it, even if it will send me to my grave.

Mama Sacketey: I mean, I just want to advise you.

She leaves for the church. Meanwhile, Doeyo is chatting with the teacher, and others are packing up. Ayeku is walking with the prophet.

Livingston: Doeyo, you seem to amaze me every day. Congratulations! That was a masterpiece, and I believe the message has been sent out.

Doeyo: Thanks so much, but I think the credit goes to God and you. I did it for my sisters at the shrine. I hope the right message has been sent.

Livingston: I know that will bring you some problems. You have to pray, and I will be praying with you. *(Observing her)* You look worried, or is the acting taking its toll on you?

Doeyo: I think I have a problem. The last time I went to the pond, the rumour I was worried about was confirmed.

Livingston: What is it?

Doeyo: You mean you don't know *(murmuring)*, if you were my agemate, I would have asked if you were a stranger in Jerusalem, as I read in the story book. *(saying out loud)* It's all over town.

Livingston: You know, I don't listen to what some of the people in this town say. But I overheard some women saying that the chief, priest, teacher Ako, and prophet, as well as Ayeku, are all struggling to betroth you as their wife. Is that true?

Doeyo: How can five people have one woman for a wife? Anyway, it is late. We can talk about this again before you leave for the big town.

SCENE 11
At the Mission House

Prophet: What do you want to discuss with me? I'm tired and would like to go to bed if it is not pressing.

Ayeku: It's good news. I know you will be happy to hear it.

Prophet: Is it about your meeting with the chief? He agreed you should take a wife, but you didn't tell him who you wanted to marry. A schoolboy with a wife, hmm!

Ayeku: *(Stunned)* How did you know? Were you listening to us? But how? Ok, the chief told you so.

Prophet: You spoke with the chief a few moments before you two came to the durbar, so how can you say the chief told me?

Ayeku: How then did you know, if I may inquire, prophet?

Prophet: If youthful arrogance were money, I would have been very rich by now. The fault is not yours. You are trying to sing the songs the elders in your family sang some time ago and are trying to pass on to you. If you don't take my advice, you will end up eating insipid meals.

Ayeku: Prophet, why are you saying this? I know I wasn't that great of a boy. But you have always had faith in me. What did I do wrong this time? So what happened? I learned my Bible verse, I cleaned God's house, and I rolled on the beach when directed.

Prophet: Yes, my son, but the curse in your family is dragging you down.

(A knock can be heard on the door; Ayeku goes to see who it is and comes back to inform the prophet that it is one of the wives of the fetish priest.)

Prophet: Let her come in. Come in, come in, my daughter *(turns to Ayeku)*. Maybe we can continue our discussion when you come to perform your duties in the church.

Mama Sacketey: How are you, Ayeku?

Ayeku: Yes, Mighty One. (Addressing the woman) I'm fine, and I hope you are well too. (He leaves.)

Prophet: Come in, my daughter; come and have a seat beside me. It's been quite a while since I last saw you.

Mama Sacketey: Good evening, prophet.

Prophet: Good evening, my daughter. How has life been treating you?

Mama Sacketey: I'm okay, but you know, I can't say the same for everyone in my household. You know how big the household is.

Prophet: I understand, which is why I always pray for your family. You are welcome.

Mama Sacketey: My husband says he would like to discuss an important issue with you, but only if you are ready to receive him.

Prophet: *(Very relaxed)* Is that why he sent you in particular? You know, everyone is welcome in the house of the Lord. He is welcome.

Mama Sacketey: Thank you very much. I'm glad you have accepted to meet him. What time would be okay for you?

Prophet: I think when the sun covers the shore next week, Tuesday will do. *(changes the topic)*. Anyway, how is your married life?

Mama Sacketey: It's been fine except for the fact that our mother- in-law, is very difficult to live with. However, I will consult you when there is a problem beyond my control. (Smiling) I hope I will be welcome.

Prophet: That will be wonderful. You need not ask.

Mama Sacketey: Thank you very much. I would like to beg your leave; my husband will not take kindly to my returning late.

Prophet: Permission granted, and may God bless you
until the next time we meet.

(On his way home, Ayeku meets Doeyo.)

Ayeku: *(In a derogative tone)* Hei, I want to talk to you!

Doeyo: Why don't you be a little more polite and call
me by my name instead of "hei"?

Ayeku: I will call you any way I want to. You are a
woman, and you are supposed to respond
to whatever I call you. Remember, I am a
royal.

Doeyo: You are mistaken; I am not that type of woman.
You better address me properly, or I will be
offended and walk off.

Ayeku: *(Angry at this point)* Such insubordination
could only have been planted in you by
that Livingston, that small-boy-big-man
you call Sir.

Doeyo: I am sure you don't intend to talk to me, so I
will take leave of you.

Ayeku: You better have it in mind that I am going to
marry you, and nothing can change that—
either me or no one else.

Doeyo: I would prefer marrying the town crier and
joining him in the blue kiosk to marrying
a man like you.

(Ayeku stands rooted to the spot, staring after her in disbelief.)

SCENE 12

At the Shrine
Where Gitters and Anger Brew

The priest is so angry he can't sit down; he keeps pacing up and down, much to the anxiety of the Trokosi ladies. (The moment he sees Mama Sacketey, he explodes.)

Priest: What kept you so long? I guess you met one of your numerous lovers on the way—an unfaithful woman.

Mama Sacketey: I wish I had one. How happy I would be sitting under an odum tree with a lot of shade instead of this pawpaw tree! Anyway, he said you are welcome anytime you are ready.

Priest: *(Very surprised with the response from the wife.)* When did you learn this kind of insolence? Such insubordination! I wonder how I managed to marry a fishwife like you. Have you also started talking to Livingston?

Mama Sacketey: When you started accusing me of being unfaithful, you began teaching me how to be insolent. *(The priest turns away in anger.)*

A month and a half later, Livingston goes around bidding everyone farewell since he is going on vacation. Doeyo's house is the last place he goes; there are tears in her eyes as she waves goodbye.

SCENE 13
At the Church
An Inconcievable End

Prophet: You are welcome.

Priest: Thank you so much. I am very happy and relieved to be here again. It's been almost twenty years since I last set foot in this shrine; I guess you would call it a sanctuary. I remember plucking mangoes from this tree *(pointing to the tree)*. You know, when we were kids, we would leave the school at midday because the late prophet usually went for a walk around that time, run to the church, and pluck all the fruits in the churchyard. I remember causing this damage to the effigy; one of the stones I threw to pluck a ripe avocado went through the window and damaged this particular effigy. Can you believe that when we came back for confession, the old prophet prayed for me and gave me bread and honey?

Prophet: I remember that incident very well. I was convulsing that day, so they sent me to the hospital in the city. When I got back,

I learned that our former headmaster had a plan to send the boys in our school to the military barracks to be disciplined. But because the old prophet has always had a father's heart, he resisted that action.

Priest: Can you believe I decided on that day I would become the next prophet? But you know these customs and traditions. That is fate for you.

Prophet: Perhaps that went in my favour. You became a very privileged priest because of customs and tradition, and I became a prophet. Everything turned out to be in our favour. I really appreciate your positive remarks about God's house. Maybe we can start since the issue is important.

Priest: Hmm. I can hear our ancestors' breath hovering around. *(A long pause)* Hmmm... A great calamity is about to befall this town. If we don't take the necessary action, the whole town will be engulfed in a calamity from which no one will escape. (He looks the prophet eyeball to eyeball.)

Prophet: What has caused the brewing of such an inordinate calamity, if I'm permitted to ask?

Priest: You see, the gods are intermediaries between us and the God you represent. Do you understand?

Prophet: A big no, and I don't think I would ever understand, but for the sake of time we can agree to disagree, so let's continue.

Priest: Okay, let's agree to disagree, but I hope you remember certain calamities that befell this town some time ago when Doeyo's mother...

Prophet: *(Rudely cuts in)* I know of natural disasters but nothing like a calamity, but if you have decided to call it by such a name, I guess we can go on.

Priest: If you put it that way *(not happy)*, it was because a lady refused to go by the rules of the gods, and her offspring is about to cause the occurrence of another catastrophe.

Prophet: How? I will appreciate a little clarity here: Is it the offspring causing the brewing of the calamity or the irresponsibility of some men with high libido in this town?

Priest: I don't understand your question, but let me try an answer, the rule laid down by the gods is about to be flouted with impunity.

Prophet: Please go right to the point since you are talking about calamity and catastrophe.

Priest: The long and short of it is that Doeyo is to marry the fetish shrine, and anything less will bring calamity to this community because this is the verdict of the gods. An enormous tragedy occurred when a similar verdict was disregarded with impunity in the past, and it is likely a similar thing is about to happen again.

Prophet: If I'm right, what you intend to say is that you are to marry Doeyo, since the shrine does not marry. And apart from you, no one can marry Doeyo.

Priest: I believe you are correct.

Prophet: What if Doeyo is not interested in you or refuses to marry you?

Priest: She can't do that. She has to marry the shrine.

Prophet: You mean you? And who is preventing you from marrying Doeyo?

Priest: Rumour has it that you, the Chief, the Teacher, and Ayeku. But tell me, I know prophets are obliged to marry only one.

Prophet: With all due respect, I do not want my name dragged into this dogfight. What if she truly loves me, Livingston, or Ayeku and refuses to marry you? Why should she marry you? Would you do the same if she happened to be your daughter? (*He paused and looked at him, eyeball to eyeball.*) Since we are dealing with rumours, rumouralso have it that she is your sister.

Priest: I guess you don't understand what I'm trying to put across.

Prophet: I'm trying hard to see if I can comprehend, but you are not making sense. Why not someone else? I know you have countless Trokosi you can swindle with this fabrication, and they will concur. Why add the poor, innocent girl?

Priest: It's custom and tradition! And this is the bedrock of our community.

Prophet: Tradition, tradition. Four teachers had to leave this town, and now the school does not have enough teachers just because they did not agree with your definition of tradition *(changes tone)*. Three young nurses vacated their posts because they refused to marry this shrine. Our health post has no permanent doctor because you have placed an embargo and issued a decree that no health personnel should stay in this town. You use your "tradition" to veto and set us back whenever this town is poised to advance. Your thinking seems to be so heavily clouded by tradition that inventions and innovations seem so far away from your home. You are keeping us all close to the shore because you are terrified of expanding horizons.

Priest: Why is it that you all seem not to understand my point of view? Why is it so difficult to understand that I am on a crusade to save this town?

Prophet: Simple, because you are retrograde, backward, and retrogressive. Anytime we move two steps forward, your house brings us seven steps backward in the name of "sankofa" and "some tradition." You seem not to be evolving with time. *(Angry now)*. It took the life of the late doctor to make female circumcision unpopular in this town. Now you are enjoying its fruits since you marry almost every other year, and I'm stuck with a lady who lies like a log, not even aware of what goes on when we are engaged in a "horizontal relationship." The torture of the grave is only known to the corpse. Your problem is that you want us all to sing along happily, even when you are playing a dirge. We are not stoics. (He gets up and straightens himself.)

Priest: *(Looking surprised at the behaviour of the prophet.)* Our ancestors delivered these customs to me, and they must be upheld. After all, it happens everywhere, even in Christendom. Don't you celebrate the Christian rituals every year?

Prophet: I do agree that some customs should be upheld, but not when the mosquito has gotten an antidote to the orange peel we burn to kill them. Our customs should be dynamic not retrogressive. Why do you apply "Sankofa" to things that are only in your interest?

Priest: So, what are you saying? If you can't see, can't you hear the gods hovering all around?

Prophet: All I'm trying to say is that we have passed the antediluvian age where ladies were forced into marriage because of some strange custom. Besides, the gods are at liberty to hover around. After all, what prevents them from landing? They should come and see what is happening to us today. I am sure they would like to bathe in the scorching sun. Priest, it seems you don't understand the times; you are becoming a nuisance, and you seem to be dancing long after the drumming has ended. Once we were children...

Just then, the chief enters the church and he is surprised to see the priest in the mission house, and, gazes surreptitiously at him.

Chief: Hello, I never knew you were busy. Anyway, I'll come later on. *(As he is about to leave,)* What are you discussing? You only use this tone of voice when preaching on Sundays.

Before the prophet can open his mouth, the teacher storms in, grumbling. He is dumbfounded by the presence of the people in the room.

Teacher: I'm very sorry for such unruly behaviour. I'm very sorry, but what has led to such a gathering and shouting?

Before the prophet could answer, the linguist burst into the church and apologised for his disorderly behaviour.

Prophet: *(He answered all.)* We were discussing the
same issue all of you came to discuss with
me.

Teacher: *(Almost shocked to the foundation of his
being.)* You mean the chief has discussed
the same issue with you?

All three: What did they discuss with you?

Prophet: The same things you all discussed with me

Teacher: This is surprising!

Prophet: Yes, it's surprising how selfishness and
greed have eaten into our established
system, and bribery and corruption have
decorated themselves with "inefficiency"
and are worn by people in high authority
in this town.

Teacher: That was interesting and intriguing; it's
been quite some time since I heard such
a thought-provoking statement. However,
when corruption and his twin brother
bribery knocked on the door of the fetish
priest and managed to enter this town,
I thought the guards in the chief's court
could stop them. Unfortunately, they were
unable to, so they multiplied, and they were
joined by their siblings, nepotism, and
favouritism, and now rule in the highest
office of the land. I hoped and prayed that
they would not enter God's house. But my
hopes have been cut short by the way I see
things.

Prophet: *(Pretending not to have heard what was said.)* May God have mercy on some people? Like my Bible says, wisdom is too lofty for the fool. Hmmm

Priest: And you, teacher, I'm always surprised at your utterances. You should know better. However, whenever you open that mouth of yours, it appears as though you speak before you ruminate. It's as if you never sucked your mother's breast. Who said corruption entered this town through my house? I wonder what you teach at the school, besides taking the children as concubines. You should have known that when "He whose name is a taboo" landed in this part of our world, it was the chiefs who sold the people, not the fetish priests. You still teach the things "He whose name is a taboo," taught you, yet you call me corrupt. The last time the grandchild of "He whose name is a taboo" visited this town, you followed him, smiling sheepishly and crisscrossing the town, engaging in unnecessary pleasantries like a politician who has just won an election. So why this provocative statement.

Chief: *(Frowns, and murmurs something)* Sacrilege, blasphemy, an abomination—you folks are acting like you never grew up around an elderly person. I don't blame you; modernization gave rise to this phenomenon. I would have counselled you to return to tradition because doing so is the first step towards progress, but once an abomination becomes established, it becomes a tradition. So why should I counsel you? Our ancestors may be turning in their graves with what is going on.

Priest: *(He ignores the chief and continues; he turns towards the prophet.)* And you, prophet, I am surprised at you. Aren't you still dressed in the clothes "He whose name is a taboo" left you? Yet you blame me for maintaining tradition. As for the chief, the less said about him, the better. He should be aware that if a snake doesn't act like one, little children will use it for firewood. If it had not been that he has royal blood flowing through him, who would have engaged such an idiot to manage even his corn mill? We were all classmates here, and who among you did he ever do better than? The shrine will marry the young lady just the same way he ascended to the throne. Truly, "Woe to the land whose chief is a youth and whose princes feast in the morning." I am sure I am quoting the scriptures better than you, prophet.

Prophet: Even the devil quoted the scriptures, "Satan himself masquerades as an angel of light," so you have said nothing, my friend.

Teacher: At least I teach them to be like "He whose name is a taboo" and not traitors like some people who invoke tradition to veto any issues they can't explain, especially if it's in their favour.

Chief: *(Very angry)* This is the most derogatory and distasteful statement I have ever heard. I thought because I'm here, my subjects would exercise some decorum, but it seems you all have no respect for authority. And who said we sabotaged our people? It was the prophet and the teacher *(he turned towards them)*. Look at the way we are all dressed. They thought dressing and walking like "He whose name is a taboo," would earn them respect. One does not achieve greatness by claiming greatness. Who among us here is dressed like "He whose name is a taboo"? In order to be accepted and liked by "He whose name is a taboo" they constantly dress, walk, talk, and behave like "He whose name is a taboo." Ironically, they continue to see themselves as inferior to "He whose name is a taboo," and they think that this is how they are perceived by them. Consequently, they are not treated as guests at his table but rather as waiters and recipients of alms. When the great-grandson of "He whose name is a taboo," as the priest correctly pointed out, paid us a visit, were they not foolishly kneeling prostrate before them? Shame on you all, traitors and conspirators! *(He swung around to face the priest.)* I find it surprising that you are still fighting over this young woman.

Priest, with all the Trokosi ladies in your shrine, I am surprised you are still fighting over this young lady.

Prophet: *(At this moment, he is boiling like hot water.)* Your highness, I believe it would be in your interest to acquaint yourself with the congregation you are addressing. We all played under that mango tree and caught crabs by the lagoon. As you correctly pointed out, one does not achieve greatness by clamouring for fame. Speaking of corruption, I'm sure you still remember how you were treated with contempt the last time the district chief executives and the auditors from the big city paid us an unexpected visit to audit our books. *(He paused.)* But as we all know, the disease runs in the family. You like to do things the way your parents did since you are their child. They were corrupt and dishonest from the start. Please clarify: weren't they the ones who took the whisky and the guns from "He whose name is a taboo"? They are as clueless about the truth as chickens are about urine. It is only understandable when your family lies, - since they are liars. I have no doubt that you will instantly disagree with what I'm saying! which, given that we are all familiar with you, is acceptable to us. *(He turned towards the teacher.)* The less said about you, teacher, the better. As for the priest, we all know his stand. The day the youth revolts, we will see the destruction of our unbending traditions.

As the four elders battled with words, with each party telling the other he should be ashamed for contemplating marrying Doeyo, footsteps could be heard outside the church. Within a moment, Doeyo's auntie bursts into the church with some elders from the town and some family members. They all seem agitated. Before the elders could ask any questions, Doeyo's aunt, Narki, collapsed. The priest sends for the nurse. The teacher starts to insult the priest and accuse him of being a fraud. Narki is revived by the nurse and starts narrating her story. The church premise is quickly turned into a palace for the chief to address the situation.

Chief: Linguist, I believe it is now necessary for us to get out of this quagmire. *(He murmured something.)* "Uneasy lies the head that wears the crown."

Linguist: Yes, Chief, I have taken my position as the linguist. I am here.

Narki: *(Still crying)* Oh, a mighty tree has fallen in our house! oh! Doeyo is no more. She has gone to the land of the silent ones. She is dead; that which is blown away by the wind will never be revived again. The sting of death is as powerful as sin. It stings the young and the old.

Chief: *(Still patronising.)* What are you saying, woman? Is it a ploy so that I don't marry your daughter?

Narki: I said, Doeyo, my daughter is dead. Selfish people!

Priest: In which context does "dead" mean what? Woman, we don't need riddles at this moment; we need answers. What happened to her? Where is she? Where is the wife of the shrine?

Prophet: You mean to tell us she is refusing to breathe?

Narki: You can say so if you wish.

Teacher: Ignorance!! I thought you were a sensible woman. We are in the middle of a war, and you called for a truce only to send us on a wild goose chase. The fact that she is not breathing doesn't mean she is dead. There's this sickness called coma that I read about in a science book for the pupil; perhaps she's in a coma.

Narki: Teacher, please don't insult my intelligence. I'm already fifty years old, and I guess I have buried enough people to know the difference between a dead person and someone who is alive.

Teacher: I'm sorry, woman. If burying a corpse equips one with the ability to diagnose death, then I think the prophet would be the best person to do that since he doesn't only bury them but also hears their "negative confessions" and undertakes their burial service.

Prophet: I believe she is not dead; I just saw her some hours ago. Woman, rest assured, I'm here.

Priest: Prophet, you are here for what? And have you forgotten what your Bible says—that two people would be grinding together and one would be taken away—or don't you study your Bible? Look at your face. I think I can be both a prophet and a fetish priest.

Narki: Maybe he will resurrect her and marry her as well. Crab devourers.

Chief: *(The whole place becomes quiet, then the chief starts laughing.)* Ye men of little faith, do you mean you are accepting the fact that she is dead?

Teacher: What else do you expect from such faithless and untrustworthy creatures? *(Turns towards the prophet.)* Prophet, do you mean you can't do anything? Aren't you a prophet of God? You have been talking about Elisha and Elijah. It's your turn. Peter and other disciples brought people back from the dead.

Prophet: Teacher, I thought you were having visions and dreams about her. Why don't you save her? After all, that is what you said you did in the vision.

Linguist: Don't mind that liar; all he knows are the stories he has been reading for the pupils at school.

Chief: At least she should have waited until after the honeymoon. She can't take all those precious assets to the grave!

Teacher: It's regrettable to have a chief who does not only eat in the morning but also becomes intoxicated before daybreak.

The chief was about to challenge the teacher when Ayeku entered with Mensa.

Ayeku: It's true she is dead; she is truly gone forever, and I mean forever.

Chief: Is he normal? Who appointed you as the local doctor? Who invited him here? *(Advancing towards Ayeku)* Are you out of your mind?

Ayeku: *(Speaking boldly.)* Uncle, I invited myself, and the youth of this town have assembled outside the churchyard ready to speak the truth to our elders. Uncle, I think your generation has let this town down. Today, there is a pervasive sense of betrayal and disillusionment, an ambiguous acceptance of an uncertain future, mixed with feelings of loss and regret.

Teacher: Do you have a history of insanity in your family? Huh! I now understand.

Linguist: Is he the guy who passed out as a doctor last year?

Chief: How dare you talk to your elders like this? (*Addressing the linguist.*) We are royals. Ayeku is a royal.

Ayeku: Doeyo's death is a mystery. This morning, I was strolling along the beach when I observed someone running in my direction. I waited a moment to see who it was, and then I saw it was Doeyo running towards me. Sadly, she tripped only a foot from me and fell into my arms. But tragically, in the process, she was pierced in the stomach by the old, corroded metal that was formerly a light pole on the beach but is now used to drag canoes. She was seriously injured. Although we hurriedly transported her to the hospital, we were forced to wait nearly the entire afternoon because the priest, with the support of you elders, had forbidden the doctor from staying in this town. By the time the doctor finally reported it, was already too late, and Doeyo was dead. Apparently, she was going to visit her grandmother in the big city and wanted to hand over a note for me to give to Livingston on his return. Mensa can confirm what I just said.

Priest: Do you honestly believe that we are children here, Ayeku? Wasn't this heinous drama staged at the durbar beneath the big Odum tree by Doeyo and the pupils? You only

added the hospital scene to assign blame
to me in order to discredit me. Why bring
up the issue of the doctor when the council
of elders made the decision? It ought to be
a shared obligation.

Teacher: Exactly, right.

Priest: *(He starts laughing aloud and continues.)* Ayeku,
you can tell our ages just by looking at your
uncle, the chief; we were once just like you.
Why would you tell this silly joke to your
elders? No puzzle or riddle will prevent
Doeyo from marrying the shrine. And
again, why did you include in your tale a
divine decree against the doctor?

Chief: Priest, at this moment, I can only save you
from yourself by calling the priest of the
neighbouring town to exorcise you from
the spirit of lust. Not just you, but the
teacher as well.

Teacher: I am not surprised by any of the ruses you
and your nephew are engaging in; you are
not helping anyone, chief. You must first
save yourself from marrying the maiden. I
am sure you are aware that I have read this
story too. I had the vision like the prophet
said, and I saved her. You or your family
member over there won't benefit from any
amount of trickery or maneuvering. And
why are you silent, prophet?

At this point, Ayeku and Mensa seek permission from the elders to address the gathering.

Ayeku: My elders, as a son of the soil and a royal, I appreciate and I am conscious of a child's position on the council of elders,that a child who respects the elderly will live long enough to benefit from that respect, because what we do for our elders, our children will do for us, and that a child among elders, converses with his ears, keeps silent when elders are talking, uses a strong mouth to blow a horn instead of a mortar, and breaks a snail's shell instead of a tortoise's. I also take into consideration our love of customs and our rich cultural heritage. While some of our diverse cultures have contributed to the progress of our town, most have remained relatively enigmatic and have fascinated this community, depriving us of many contemporary conveniences. Our culture has endured all adversity and weathered all storms because it is deeply ingrained in us, despite some encouraging trends to halt some of these destructive cultural practices. But when our elders decide to pick a quarrel on a market day with the youth over who should procure the last bottle of hair dye, we must not only question the town maidens about what they have been grumbling to the elders about behind closed doors but also question our elders about their aversion to wisdom. It's disappointingly despicable and dishearteningly disgusting to watch our elders' somersault over each other to outdo themselves to win Doeyo. Though I have been accused of exhibiting frivolous behaviour by every one of you since Livingston walked into this town, every single one of you has for some time now been behaving like a petulant child who has been told they can't have the mango being sold at Mama Doe's shop.

I was shocked to learn that the fish's rot begins at the head in one of the books I picked out from Livingston's library, but you've proven the author was right. As elders, you have plotted and colluded to sell nearly everything to "He whose name is a taboo," so recklessly depleting all our natural resources. And for what purpose? You use the money to deprive the young people of the chance to marry any maiden in this town. All of you elders gathered here, except for the Prophet, have an average of ten official wives and an endless number of concubines. The youth waiting outside, I'm sure, think that your names should rather be a "taboo on our lips."

Linguist: My son, you are making sense, but a point of correction: I just have seven wives.

Ayeku: Keep quiet, linguist. I said an average of ten wives. I never understood Mensa, Doeyo, or Livingston at first, but wisdom has taught me that the same idiotic pupils we sit next to in class are the ones that grow up to be adults.

Mensa: *(Continued from where Ayeku ended)* To restate Ayeku's position, our elders: I am also deeply disappointed in all of you. The institution of customary tradition was once held in high esteem since it was the moral epicenter of the community and the salt and light of society. Unfortunately, due mostly to you, our elders, there has been an avalanche of change in the status of our "customs and traditions" in this community, with its influence and power declining and eroding each day. Paradoxically, morality has become outdated in this town, especially among the elderly. You have lost your moral compass. Our community desperately needs a moral compass that points in the direction of integrity, not the deception and filth that you, our elders, have been engaging in.

You have lost the moral struggle, elders. This community is headed for catastrophe because you, who should be using your blood to protect and guide this moral compass, have allowed it to become so broken that there doesn't seem to be any chance for it to be healed. You, our elders, are the ones who consistently demonstrate how averse you are to wisdom, not the youth.

He continued.

> How can we periodically realign the moral compass of our "customs and traditions" such that it guards and guides this town? How do we revive the "customs and traditions" whose moral foundation has crumbled so much that it cannot support this town any longer? As young people in our community, we have chosen to assume the helm of our ship and forge a new course in order to address this challenge. My elders, this is a paraphrase from one of the books I borrowed from Livingston.

Ayeku: *(Chimes in again.)* It saddens me to inform my elders that "compromise," not youth and modernization, poses the greatest threat to our "customs and traditions." Our "customs and traditions," reminiscent of the parable of the boiling frog from teacher Livingston's book: The assurance is that our "customs and traditions," like a frog plunged abruptly into boiling water, will leap out; nevertheless, if submerged in tepid water and gradually raised to a boil, it will not sense the danger and will be cooked to death. Our "customs and traditions" in this community are now in this precarious state. It keeps compromising, and the people who have been compromising our "customs and traditions" are you, our elders.

Chief: This is excellent and thought-provoking, though derogatory; I think Livingston has done a good job.

Prophet: I think I must review my notes on Livingston. I am overwhelmed with your submission.

Teacher: Why only Livingston? Before he arrived, wasn't I here?

Ayeku: Prophet, you've truly disappointed me. I was shocked to see a passage that so eloquently portrayed the town's leaders in the Bible I borrowed from Livingston. Let me paraphrase: "My watchmen" cannot see anything. They do not know anything. They are all like dogs that cannot make a noise. They cannot make the noise that dogs usually make. They lie, and they dream. They like to sleep. They are like dogs that like to eat a lot. And they never have enough. They are like sheep who do not understand anything. They all turn to doing what they want. Everybody tries to get what they can for themselves. They shout, 'Come! We must get wine! We must drink as much beer as we can! And tomorrow will be like today. It might be much better!" It was surprising to me that, despite having this book for so long, all you asked us to do was roll on the beach.

Prophet: That is excellent. I am very proud of Livingston and am not being sarcastic here.

Just then, the leader of the youth association that Livingston set up walked in, bowed his head, and requested to make a comment on behalf of the youth of the town. He then pulled out an "official paper" from his pocket that contained extracts from articles he had borrowed from Livingston.

Youth Leader: I ask your elders to please listen to me. Mama Kai, the magistrate court's porridge vendor, is my mother. I am her eldest son. My language isn't as sweet-smelling and deodorised as Ayeku and Mensa's because I'm not royalty. In case I come across as impolite, please accept my apologies and treat me like a suckling child. I think it's best for this town that I'm outraged. Our people say that although the mouth of our elders may be without teeth, it's never without words of wisdom, since the strength of the elderly is in the ears and lips. However, it's becoming increasingly difficult to use this adage to describe our elders these days.

Our elders seem to be suffering from blurred and impaired vision and are plagued by a twin virus: ruminating on the past and petty jealousies. Sadly, we, the youth in this town, have not called you out on these. Consequently, there hasn't been enough scorn and contempt for your incompetence. For some time now, you have encouraged the system of patronage. You have flippantly rewarded mediocrity inanely while tossing meritocracy to the wolves. You have encouraged nepotism, which has taken hold in this town like wildfire, by using culture and royalty. Regrettably, the town's underdevelopment is the price of your nepotism. These same members of the royal family presently hold every sought-after jobs in this town, even though everyone knows that persons of royal ancestry are born on top of the anthill. The absurdity of the situation is heightened by the fact that none of them are qualified for the positions they have been given, save for the fact that they are members of the royal family.

Not just that, you have permitted and perpetuated a pretty irritating infiltration of this system with sentimental sympathy and a biassed thinking capacity that forbids dissenting and divergent dialogue. Competition for this young maiden has worsened the situation. You, who are supposed to be "brainware" for the community, have failed to find an antidote to our problems but are rather engrossed and outdoing yourselves to win the heart of Doeyo.

I apologise, but it seems to the young people in this town that your moral compass is irreparably damaged, and that you are making decisions based on your waist rather than your intellect.

He continued....

You have failed to remind yourselves that even the best dancers on the stage must retire sometime and are frivolously paying the dowry of the maidens in this town to the detriment of the youth. Though you don't say it, we know you live by the values of, "no matter how full the river, it must still grow." Is it surprising that this whole town has become a crime scene? Paradoxically, it's the same criminals who are supervising the search for those who committed the crime. You have nurtured bribery and corruption, forgetting that when one feeds a lion cub vegetable, it doesn't deter it from eating meat as it transitions to adulthood. Today, bribery and corruption have grown at an alarming rate. (He pointed at them.) Which of you cares about the development of this town that is bedeviled with rampant poverty? Like rain, poverty has drenched us all in this town equally.

In addition to the high unemployment rate in this town, those of us who do have jobs earn low wages that are insufficient to sustain our families and dependents, which forces many of us to turn to bribes to meet our basic needs. Today, corruption in this town extends beyond the simple act of receiving bribes and has become a pervasive state of mind and way of life, even at the chief's palace and other locations of power. The attitude has evolved from trying to "make ends meet" to one of entitlement by people in positions of power and authority, even our elders. Our elders have failed to understand that corruption extends beyond the wonton stealing and sale of our town's resources but also involves taking advantage of our young maidens and putting bad people in high-profile positions who lack the skills and drive to execute the job. How many of our young women are currently enrolled in one of our few struggling high schools?

My elders, you have failed to set the example that all others must follow. The result of this is what we are seeing today. It's said that a town without the elderly is like a well without water. The youth in this town want to cultivate friendship with the elderly, so like trees, we will have roots, but unfortunately, our elders have developed a penchant for patronising the market and therefore have lost every respect. Instead of erecting yourselves as boundaries for this town, you have become a sledgehammer being used to breakdown every barrier our ancestors sacrificed their blood to build for us.

Ayeku: *(He pauses and turns towards the chief.)* The story of Doeyo sounds like what you told me: Doeyo is a hero like no other.

As stunned as they are, they can only open their mouths in shame and disappointment.

Ayeku: Before she died, she gave me this note and made me swear never to give it to anybody but Livingston.

(After some deliberations, they all departed in shame.)

SCENE 14

At Doeyo's House and on the street

A month later, Livingston returned from vacation. On reaching the town, he meets Doeyo's aunt as he gets out of the vehicle.

Narki: You are welcome, my son. I hope you had a nice vacation.

Livingston: Thank you. Yes, my vacation was restful.

Narki: Doeyo left a note for you.

Livingston: Why? Where is she?

Narki: She's gone.

Livingstone: Gone where? When is she coming back?

Narki: She is not coming back; stop asking me these questions.

Livingston: Why? Has she been excommunicated? I had a premonition, and I knew something would go wrong when I was about to leave for my vacation. By the way, where has she gone? Maybe I can secretly visit her.

Narki: *(Almost weeping.)* Well, she's gone to the land of the silent ones; there's only one route that leads to the place, and no one has ever returned from it.

Livingston: *(Forgetting he is carrying luggage, he follows Doeyo's aunt.)* I think I will seek the chief's permission and visit her.

Narki: The chief has no power over her; nobody has apart from God.

Livingston: I know that *(still not aware of what was going on),* so why are you pulling my legs? I would like to see Doeyo; I bought her a present.

Narki: Why are you trying to remind me of my sorrows? *(She goes in and brings him a letter.)*

Ayeku walks in at the same time and gives him another letter. When he started reading theletter, he couldn't control the tears, just like Doeyo's aunt.

He leaves Doeyo's aunt's place and walks on the street, crying. (The whole town gathers around him, including the chief, the teacher, and the prophet, as if there is a durbar, and in a loud cry he addresses them.)

Livingston: You are all looking, yes, like a tradition once again, as another human's life is lost because Doeyo wanted to teach the "unteachable and greedy" how to be selfless.

She is no more, and I guess this is normal for you in this town. But how many more people will have to lose their lives for you to learn? *(The whole place becomes quiet as everyone listens, he continued).* However, she requested only one thing from those who say they love her: Trokosi and female circumcision should be abolished. She is pleading with her blood, and I hope those who say they love her will do this in her memory.

Livingston leaves them; on his way home, he goes to sit on the tombstone where he used to sit with Doeyo during his free time. As if to talk to the latter, he takes the letters again, and as he reads, he finds boldly written underneath one of them, "Thank you for putting my hand in that of God's. Though in suffering, my soul is at peace with God.

A year later, the chief and the elders passed a law abolishing the practice of Trokosi and female circumcision in the town, but like any long-practiced custom, some die-hard practitioners still do it on the quiet.

9 789988 376475